COLLABORATIVE TEAMS THAT WORK

The Definitive Guide to Cycles of Learning in a PLC

Colin Sloper and Gavin Grift

Foreword by Anthony Muhammad

Solution Tree | Press

a division of
Solution Tree

American version published in the United States by Solution Tree Press

555 North Morton Street
Bloomington, IN 47404
800.733.6786 (toll free) / 812.336.7700
FAX: 812.336.7790

email: info@SolutionTree.com
SolutionTree.com

Visit **go.SolutionTree.com/PLCbooks** to download the free reproducibles in this book.

Printed in the United States of America

Library of Congress Cataloging-in-Publication Data

Names: Sloper, Colin, author. | Grift, Gavin, author.
Title: Collaborative teams that work : the definitive guide to cycles of
    learning in a PLC / Colin Sloper, Gavin Grift.
Description: Bloomington, IN : Solution Tree Press, [2021] | Includes
    bibliographical references and index.
Identifiers: LCCN 2021020737 (print) | LCCN 2021020738 (ebook) | ISBN
    9781951075897 (paperback) | ISBN 9781951075903 (ebook)
Subjects: LCSH: Professional learning communities. | Teachers--Professional
    relationships. | Teachers--In-service training. | Teaching teams. |
    Reflective teaching. | Action research in education. | School
    improvement programs.
Classification: LCC LB1731 .S5258 2021 (print) | LCC LB1731 (ebook) | DDC
    370.71/1--dc23
LC record available at https://lccn.loc.gov/2021020737
LC ebook record available at https://lccn.loc.gov/2021020738

Solution Tree
Jeffrey C. Jones, CEO
Edmund M. Ackerman, President

Solution Tree Press
President and Publisher: Douglas M. Rife
Associate Publisher: Sarah Payne-Mills
Art Director: Rian Anderson
Managing Production Editor: Kendra Slayton
Copy Chief: Jessi Finn
Production Editor: Alissa Voss
Content Development Specialist: Amy Rubenstein
Copy Editor: Alissa Voss
Proofreader: Evie Madsen
Text and Cover Designer: Abigail Bowen
Editorial Assistants: Sarah Ludwig and Elijah Oates

Collaborative Teams That Work: The Definitive Guide to Cycles of Learning in a PLC originally published in Australia by Hawker Brownlow Education

© 2020 Hawker Brownlow Education

Thank you for participating in one of our professional learning workshops! We hope that you found the workshop valuable! For additional professional learning, please enjoy the book that continues our focus on impactful educational practices.

We look forward to seeing you at another session!

Pam and Karen

Acknowledgments

A book such as this would be impossible to write without drawing on our privileged experience of working with countless schools, collaborative teams, school leaders, and educators since 2010. Their commitment to the professional learning community (PLC) process and their unrelenting focus on improving their students' learning have enabled us to learn alongside them and identify through action research the key actions that need to be the focus of collaborative teams' collective endeavors. This has certainly been a case of learning by doing.

We would also like to acknowledge those pioneers who have had such a monumental influence on our thinking and practices. Richard and Rebecca DuFour were foundational in the introduction of PLCs to our professional lives, and their impact could not be more pronounced. The legacy they have left for schools, teachers, and students is truly exceptional. Tammy Heflebower was instrumental in sparking conversations that led to us working with some of the most credible research in the field of education, that of Robert J. Marzano, which then led to the publication of this book.

The Thinking Collaborative™ community continues to offer educators a unique and critically important way of thinking about how they engage in their work, and this has influenced us both greatly. All the PLC at Work® training associates we have had the pleasure of working alongside have helped to shape our thinking, approaches, and ideology in the PLC arena. Particular thanks to Janet Malone, Austin Buffum, Terri L. Martin, Anthony Muhammad, and Tim Brown for their inspiration, insight, and expertise in sharing the PLC at Work process, all of which has been influential to our thinking and work.

Lastly, it is important to acknowledge the Australian PLC associates with whom we have worked. They have contributed to the PLC field in Australia and made valuable contributions to our thinking along the way.

Visit **go.SolutionTree.com/PLCbooks** to download the free reproducibles in this book.

Table of Contents

About the Authors

Colin Sloper has been a teacher, an assistant principal, and a principal in Australian government schools since 1983. In the course of his career, he has been involved in the establishment of five new state government schools, including his time as principal of Pakenham Springs Primary School in Victoria, Australia. Through his leadership and collaborative work with the school community, Pakenham Springs became the first recognized model of a PLC in Australia.

As a school leader, Colin has specialized in growing new schools by building a learning-focused culture throughout the school community. His leadership has emphasized student engagement while achieving substantial results for both the students and teachers he has served. Colin's schools are highly sought after as sites of professional learning for staff across all educational sectors.

Gavin Grift is the founder and CEO of *Grift Education* (https://grifteducation.com). His passion, commitment, humor, and highly engaging style have made him one of Australia's most in-demand presenters.

He has held numerous educational leadership positions throughout his career and led the development of PLC networks across Australia, culminating in the establishment of the Centre for Professional Learning Communities (https://cpl.asn.au), informed by the work and legacies of Richard and Rebecca DuFour.

Gavin is coauthor of numerous articles and best-selling books, including *Five Ways of Being: What Learning Leaders Think, Do, and Say Every Day*; *Teachers as Architects of Learning: Twelve Constructs to Design and Configure Successful Learning Experiences*; *Collaborative Teams That Transform Schools: The Next Step in PLCs*; *Transformative Collaboration: Five Commitments for Leading a Professional Learning Community*; and the revised Australian edition of *Learning by Doing: A Handbook for Professional Learning Communities at Work®*.

To learn more about Gavin's work, follow @GGrift on Twitter and LinkedIn, or @grifteducation on Facebook.

Preface

Experts by Experience

We first came across the term *experts by experience* when reading *The Kindness Method: Changing Habits for Good Using Self-Compassion and Understanding* by Shahroo Izadi (2018). In her introduction, Izadi (2018) states, "The field of addiction recovery widely acknowledges the wisdom of 'experts by experience'—people who've been there before us and done it. I am writing *The Kindness Method* partly as a practitioner, but mainly as an expert by experience" (p. 10).

Just as in the field of addiction therapy, the field of education widely acknowledges the importance of experts by experience: those practitioners who support and lead others through transformational change, having been there and done it for themselves. That's what we bring to this book. Our ideas, approaches, and subsequent advice is based on over twenty years of working together, and over a decade of leading and supporting schools to become high-functioning and successful professional learning communities (PLCs).

We have worked in schools across Australia, New Zealand, and Southeast Asia—sometimes in the same school, sometimes in different schools. We have worked with government, church-run, and independent school systems and schools, from small rural elementary schools to secondary schools that are bursting at the seams and everything in between. Through these varied experiences, we have observed firsthand many of the challenges that schools face in their efforts to cultivate a collaborative culture. In supporting schools through these challenges, we have engaged with leadership, grade-level, specialist, cross-discipline, faculty, and department teams. Much of this work has been to assist these teams in ensuring their collaborative efforts strengthen curriculum and assessment, and ultimately to transform their instructional practices to improve learning outcomes.

Where It Started for Us

Influential to our commitment to PLC at Work® was the privilege of being involved in bringing the process to Australian schools. Working closely with Richard and Rebecca DuFour, we led the implementation of PLCs in Australian schools through three pilot programs over four years, and in 2014 established the Centre for Professional Learning Communities, which has since become part of the PLC support now provided by Hawker Brownlow Education. In the years since, the school Colin led as principal became the first national model of a PLC, while many other schools across Australia embraced higher levels of teacher collaboration through a clearly articulated and operationalized mission and vision to ensure high levels of student achievement for all.

As we traveled from school to school, we observed that common patterns of implementation confusion and uncertainty were making the PLC journey challenging. These issues ranged from a lack of understanding about what becoming a PLC would truly mean for everyone involved to staff blatantly resisting any change to the status quo.

Having supported a diverse range of teams from different backgrounds and experiences to implement the collaborative process, we have developed significant expertise in assisting schools to overcome these challenges while taking into account their own unique characteristics and contexts. Armed with firsthand knowledge of the tools, priorities, and approaches that work for schools—and those that do not—it is now time for us to share this expertise.

Influences on This Work

Along with the experience gained from learning by doing, this work also draws from the experiences of many generous and talented educators we've worked with over the years. Their thoughts, ideas, and processes, and the way they've translated ideas into action, have been influential as we have trialed, modified, and strengthened the cycle of learning process detailed in the pages that follow.

We also acknowledge the influence of both the Cognitive Coaching℠ and Adaptive Schools programs on our thinking. These bodies of work detail the necessary skills and provide educators with tools for high-level collaboration. In writing *Collaborative Teams That Work*, we were mindful to not just create another book telling educators about the work that needs to be done. Instead, we have focused on the processes through which schools can foster a safe and supportive team culture, where educators can develop and strengthen their skills of working collaboratively as they actually do the work.

We are privileged to have worked alongside some of the world's leading researchers and practitioners in the field of PLCs, and this has heavily influenced our understanding of the actions collaborative teams must carry out. In particular, the PLC at Work process has provided us with a genuine means of supporting schools in fundamentally changing the way they "do" school (DuFour, DuFour, Eaker, Many, & Mattos, 2016). We believe no other process that we've read, researched, or seen in practice is as effective as when the PLC at Work process is implemented with fidelity and steadfast commitment. Having said that, we have written this book in part to fill the gap in the literature about the specific actions collaborative teams take when schools engage in this work earnestly.

Closely aligned with our PLC endeavors has been our work with Robert J. Marzano and his colleagues at Marzano Resources in the areas of collaboration, instruction, and assessment, and in the publication of *Collaborative Teams That Transform Schools: The Next Step in PLCs* (Marzano, Heflebower, Hoegh, Warrick, & Grift, 2016). This body of work provided us with further impetus to assist teams to achieve the ultimate goal of higher levels of learning for the students they serve. The very title of the book suggests that it is the collaborative teams themselves that are the key drivers for sustained cultural and structural change. This work, in particular, sharpened our focus on assisting schools to monitor their efforts in improving teaching practice and student learning as well as to understand the importance of leadership to the success of teams' collective efforts.

The Marzano High Reliability Schools™ framework put forward in *A Handbook for High Reliability Schools: The Next Step in School Reform* (Marzano, Warrick, & Simms, 2014) has also been influential in our work with schools. With over forty years of school-improvement research to draw from, this work reiterates the power of the PLC at Work process as a catalyst for deep, sustainable change in schools and highlights the importance of building a safe and supportive psychological space for successful collaboration.

In 2016, we contributed to *Transformative Collaboration: Five Commitments for Leading a Professional Learning Community* alongside our colleagues Tonia Flanagan, Kylie Lipscombe, and Janelle Wills. Drawing from our collective expertise and with a foreword by Alma Harris and Michelle Jones, *Transformative Collaboration* assists schools to build the leadership capacity necessary to successfully manage their school's transformation into a PLC. The professional learning we subsequently provided in support of this work highlighted, "warts and all," how essential it is that leaders truly connect with the PLC process and genuinely accept that it can—and will—transform student and teacher learning.

These key works, combined with our ongoing collaboration with each other to find the most effective ways of supporting schools to become PLCs, led us to write this book. However, we didn't want to fall into the trap of spending the majority of our time admiring the problem and precious little time addressing it. Our approach with *Collaborative Teams That Work* has instead been to practice what we preach in schools: take the time necessary to identify problems but spend the majority of our time inquiring about solutions.

Foreword

By Anthony Muhammad

School improvement is such a hotly debated topic. Everyone involved with this debate recognizes that the proper intellectual and social development of our students is the key to the prosperity of our society. I do not believe that anyone disagrees that schools can and must improve; any debate or disagreement must surely lie in how to accomplish this end. Should we extend the school year? Should we reduce class size? Should we increase school funding? Should we evaluate teachers more rigorously? So many opinions, but very few definitive answers can be found.

I struggled with this reality of school improvement as a new principal in 2001. I wondered if I should prescribe the teachers' duties and behaviors like an autocrat, or whether I should sit back and help the teachers *discover* what is best for their students. The answer came when I attended a PLC at Work® event in Lincolnshire, Illinois, in July that year. After attending this event, the evidence was clear: placing teachers into strong collaborative teams where they would engage in a process of continuous inquiry about their practice was the answer.

Once I returned to my school site, the *idea* and the *reality* of implementation were worlds apart. The speakers cited the research effortlessly and made the process sound so easy, and I had a vision of the type of healthy collaboration that was necessary to improve student performance, but there was no road map for leading the process. This lack of a clear path to creating strong collaborative teams resulted in a lot of mistakes and delays in improvement. In the beginning, I monitored the wrong work, constructed the teams improperly, and gathered the wrong artifacts. There was research and guidance available from the business community, but schools are unique entities. I felt as if we were building an airplane midflight.

Some of the questions that caused me to take pause included the following.

- What proof should I gather to verify good collaboration, and what is a fair standard of excellence?
- How involved should I be as a leader?

- How quickly should I expect teams to improve, and how much patience should I exercise?

- How should I respond to saboteurs and process resisters?

- How much time and how many resources should we invest to promote team growth?

As a leader, I knew that my contribution to school improvement was to develop, support, and monitor strong collaborative teams of teachers. It took years of trial and error before our culture changed and we began to truly work collaboratively. This relentless focus helped our school evolve from a model of school failure to a lighthouse of educational achievement. Our school earned several local and national awards for excellence in student achievement, and in 2005 I was honored as the Michigan Middle School Principal of the Year. In my acceptance speech, I thanked my teachers for accepting the challenge to work collaboratively because, as a principal, I did not prepare one lesson, deliver one formative student assessment, or provide one academic intervention; this was the work of the team. My effectiveness as a leader rested in my ability to break down the walls of isolation and create an environment where students could benefit from their teachers' collective wisdom. This is the greatest contribution a school leader can make to improving educator effectiveness. Still, I always wondered, "What would we have accomplished if our learning curve could have been shortened?"

The University of Chicago Consortium on School Research came to a similar conclusion about the role of the principal in school improvement (Allensworth & Hart, 2018). In a 2018 report on school improvement, which included studying the progress of over six hundred low-performing elementary schools for eight years (2007–2014), the schools that made remarkable progress improved under the guidance of a leader who created the following professional culture:

1. *Successful principals develop systems for supporting teachers to support students . . .*

2. *Successful principals are skilled in organizing and supporting shared leadership among staff . . .*

3. *Successful principals manage shared leadership by guiding, coordinating, and monitoring the work of teachers and leaders in the school. (Allensworth & Hart, 2018, p. 4)*

It took me six years to figure out for myself what *Collaborative Teams That Work* explains as a logical and effective multistage process. This book is a gift to anyone who wants to support the development of strong collaborative teams but simply does not have access to the insight on how to do it.

Gavin Grift and Colin Sloper have provided practitioners with a guide that I would have given my right arm to have access to in 2001. The worlds of research and practice are more in harmony in 2021 than ever before in the history of our profession. Study after study implores schools to set up conditions that produce strong collaborative teams that engage in continuous cycles of the *right* work: curriculum, instruction, assessment, intervention, and enrichment.

I encourage anyone who has access to this book to read it carefully and apply the lessons that are so masterfully laid out in what is a brilliant, research-based manifesto on producing the most valuable asset in any effective school: strong collaborative teams. Schools are institutions, and their educators are not islands. The more we harness the power of *we*, the less we will understand why we ever chose to work in isolation.

Introduction

This book sets out an evidence-based process that collaborative teams can use to genuinely improve the achievement of all students in their schools. Never before has there been such consensus on the elements that improve schools and student learning. While each school's unique context cannot be ignored, research highlights that a genuine focus on creating highly impactful collaborative teams must sit at the heart of any school- or system-improvement agenda (DuFour et al., 2016). Research also indicates that teaching practice has the biggest influence on improving learning for students, outside of the students themselves (Hattie, 2012). The way to maximize this influence is to cultivate a collaborative culture where educators support one another to deeply examine their impact through focused inquiry and deliberate action. Such a culture leads to a genuine desire in teachers to evolve their professional practice to ensure all students succeed.

The action research that collaborative teams engage in forms the basis for job-embedded professional learning and is central to enhancing teaching practice. The cycle of learning process, which we've broken down into twelve actions in this book, is the most effective way to ensure that the work of collaborative teams continually enhances individual and collective teaching practice through job-embedded action research. We want teachers to leave every collaborative team meeting considerably more skillful in relation to their teaching practice than when they arrive. The twelve key actions that we describe in the following pages underpin the cycle of learning process and guarantee that each meeting becomes a focused professional learning experience for all team members, supporting and enhancing their shared responsibility for the learning of the students they serve.

The cycle of learning process and twelve actions address the research regarding the impact that collective teacher efficacy has on student learning (Hattie, 2015). As teachers work through the cycle of learning process that we detail in this book, they will begin to identify successes, recognize difficulties as opportunities to learn, and experience their colleagues' support as they enhance their individual and collective teaching practice. Implementation of the twelve actions and associated tasks supports the development of collective teacher efficacy and strengthens team members' shared belief that they can influence student outcomes in a positive way through collective action.

1

As collaborative team members begin to see the impact of their actions on student learning, many of their entrenched beliefs about teaching and learning will be challenged and, as student learning continues to improve, change over time. Understanding from this experience that they have a greater influence on student learning than external factors, collaborative team members will realize that they are able to overcome these factors by focusing their action and work on what they *are* able to control: strengthening their teaching practice.

Professional Learning Communities

The PLC at Work process challenges school leaders and educators to view the work of PLCs as a whole-school commitment (DuFour, DuFour, Eaker, Many, & Mattos, 2016). Concurring with Richard DuFour, Rebecca DuFour, Robert Eaker, Thomas W. Many, & Mike Mattos (2016), we see schools themselves—not just the teams that serve them—as PLCs. This position ensures that there is a whole-school focus and intensifies collective efforts on building a schoolwide culture to support the work of collaborative teams. DuFour and his colleagues (2009) use the following artfully constructed and deceptively simple definition of a *PLC* as the foundation of their PLC at Work process:

> *Educators committed to working collaboratively in ongoing processes of collective inquiry and action research to achieve better results for the students they serve. (p. 14)*

This definition articulates the fundamental purpose of a PLC, and we acknowledge the power of these words and the complexity of the concepts that they embrace. It also specifies how the work of PLCs needs to be done—both at the whole-school level and at the collaborative-team level—if the school is to be successful in its transformation into a PLC.

In our years of working with schools, we have often seen schools and teams jump ahead to answer the critical PLC questions (outlined in the coming pages), bypassing this definition in their haste to get on with the work. This shifts their focus away from the true purpose of the PLC at Work process, which is to improve teaching practice and ensure high levels of learning for *all* students.

We have also seen school leaders and educators interpret this definition differently, with the unfortunate effect of creating divisions and uncertainty. Recognizing the power of a clear, succinct definition and drawing from our experiences of seeing the original definition misinterpreted or ignored, we offer the following clearly derivative version of DuFour and his colleagues' (2009) definition of a PLC, one that we hope evolves and strengthens understanding:

> *Educators committed to working collaboratively using action research in recurring collective cycles of learning to inquire into and increase the impact of their teaching practice to achieve better results for the students they serve.*

In this modified definition, we emphasize the importance of developing a collaborative culture; frame the work of teams as recurring, collective cycles of learning; position the use of action research as the best method of inquiring into and improving teaching practice; and highlight the link between improved teaching practice and improved student learning. We believe that this definition describes not only the way PLCs work but also the work of collaborative teams within a PLC.

The purpose of *Collaborative Teams That Work* is to make crystal clear the focus and work of collaborative teams within the larger framework of a PLC. To ensure this clarity, we further define the words that we have consciously used in our definition of a PLC.

Committed

Committed means having such a belief in something that you are willing to devote your time and energy to carrying it into action. In essence, being committed means being true to your word, even when doing so gets hard or you no longer feel like it.

Collaboration

The definition of *collaboration* offered by DuFour and his colleagues (2016) in *Learning by Doing* can't be beaten. In this context, collaboration is as follows:

> A systematic process in which [people] work together, interdependently, to analyze and impact their professional practice in order to improve individual and collective results. (p. 60)

Action Research

To define *action research*, we draw on the work of Richard Sagor (2000), who specifies that action research is a "disciplined process of inquiry conducted by and for those taking the action. The primary reason for engaging in action research is to assist the 'actor' in improving or refining his or her actions" (p. 3).

Cycle of Learning

Schools refer to the lessons they deliver in different ways, including *unit of instruction, learning phase, unit of work,* and *teaching program.* We use the term *cycle of learning* to refer to a unit of instruction that focuses on a particular sequence of teaching, usually focused on delivering the skills, knowledge, or dispositions related to a prioritized standard or standards. We deliberately use the word *learning* in this term to remind team members that the outcome of these cycles is educator *and* student learning.

Recurring Collective Cycles of Learning

We define *recurring collective cycles of learning* as a team's repeated implementation of action research to continually identify, investigate, and implement the best teaching practices to improve student learning. What is learned from each cycle of learning impacts when the process is repeated. Practices that prove to be highly impactful should be carried into the next cycle of learning and become part of the pedagogy of the individual and team.

Teaching Practice

We define *teaching practice* as the instructional strategies, approaches, and behaviors teachers use through the teaching and learning process. One of the major outcomes of the recurring cycle of learning process is continuous monitoring of and inquiry into the impact of teaching practice on student learning.

Inquire

In the cycle of learning process, to *inquire* means to ask questions, investigate, explore, and examine evidence to determine which teaching practices have the greatest impact on student learning. It requires an open mind, a curious spirit, and a belief in the capacity of both educators and students to learn and improve continually.

We also recognize and acknowledge the importance of the three big ideas that, according to DuFour and his colleagues (2016), underpin the PLC at Work process and support the development of a healthy school culture that assists the work of collaborative teams. These three ideas, which our modified definition of a PLC complements, follow.

1. A relentless focus on learning
2. The cultivation of a collaborative culture
3. An orientation toward results

These big ideas not only support the work of collaborative teams but also assist in establishing a strong foundation that allows teams to address the four critical PLC questions that broadly frame their work. The four critical PLC questions from the PLC at Work process are as follows.

1. What do we want our students to learn?
2. How will we know our students are learning?
3. How will we respond when some students do not learn?
4. How will we extend the learning for students who are already proficient? (DuFour et al., 2016)

These questions can be a blessing or a curse depending on the way that they are interpreted and used. They certainly assist by providing some guidance about the legitimate work of a collaborative team. However, the questions are often adopted as specific agenda items with teams not understanding that they instead represent major phases or considerations of the action research process.

We strongly believe that rather than superficially answer these questions and tick them off their to-do lists, high-performing collaborative teams focus on doing the right work to answer these questions thoughtfully. This of course then raises the question, What is the right work?

That question is the focus of this book.

The Twelve Actions Taken in a Cycle of Learning by Collaborative Teams That Work

This book outlines twelve main actions carried out in a cycle of learning by highly successful collaborative teams that have embraced the four critical questions of PLC at Work to improve their teaching practice. Implemented through each cycle of learning, these actions can help teams to scaffold their inquiry and action research to ensure students and teachers benefit from the learnings each action brings.

For a team that has been established based on the delivery of common content—be that a grade-level or faculty team—the twelve actions are as follows.

1. Map the learning pathway.
2. Prepare the preassessment.
3. Administer the preassessment.
4. Respond to identified student learning needs.
5. Design the learning program.
6. Implement the learning program.
7. Monitor the impact of instruction.
8. Analyze which instructional practices are having the greatest impact.
9. Adopt the most impactful instructional practices.
10. Administer the postassessment.
11. Determine the team's impact on student learning.
12. Action the team's learnings.

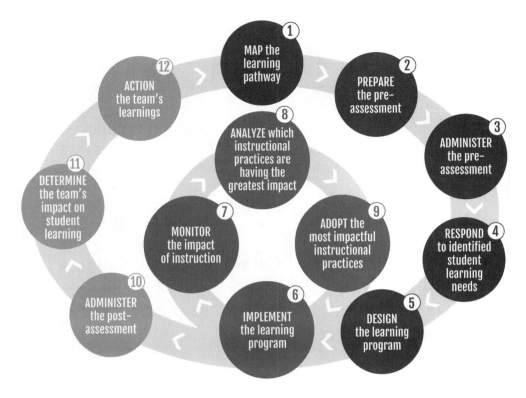

Figure I.1: The twelve actions taken in a cycle of learning by collaborative teams that work.

Using This Book

The first three sections of *Collaborative Teams That Work* explore each of these twelve actions for preparing, implementing, and reviewing learning within the cycle of learning process, noting whether the action is to be carried out in the classroom or collaborative team meetings, explaining the associated tasks, and pre-empting any challenges that may arise.

As we've noted, teams that share responsibility for delivering common content have the greatest alignment in the tasks they carry out collaboratively. The majority of this book is, therefore, devoted to the twelve actions we advocate these teams undertake. However, we acknowledge that not all teams can be formed in this ideal way. For this reason, in the fourth section of this book we provide an alternative set of eleven actions specifically to support other types of teams—for example, specialist teams, school-improvement teams, action teams, and faculty teams—to collaborate at high levels on work that aligns with our definition of a PLC.

Finally, in section 5, we bring all the elements of the cycle of learning process together. This includes sharing a process to ensure meetings are effective through the development of a targeted and concise meeting agenda. We also provide specific tips for school leaders to maximize the success of the collaborative teams they support.

This book explores a mature and high-functioning process, meaning schools and teams might not necessarily start their journey by implementing all of the suggested actions and associated tasks at once. Our aim is simply to provide a clear guide for the work of collaborative teams. It is hoped that schools will audit their teams' current work against this guide so that each team can identify which actions and tasks might comprise its next steps forward in becoming a high-performing and impactful collaborative team.

While this book shows a way forward, it is vital that schools and teams view cycles of learning within their own contexts. For example, depending on the complexity of the skills, knowledge, and dispositions in focus, team members' experiences in implementing the collaborative process, and the time available to them, some collaborative actions may take more than one meeting to work through, while it may also be possible to complete several other actions in a single meeting. Taking into account the unique situation of their school and team and each individual cycle of learning, leaders and educators should adjust the work to suit their particular needs, making modifications that represent minor diversions rather than major detours from the route to success.

We strongly believe that high-performing collaborative teams are made up of problem solvers who use the inquiry process to overcome challenges that arise. They have a genuine desire to get better at the work and to support their teams in their important quest to achieve high levels of learning for all. We view this book as a companion resource for these problem solvers that they will not only use to set up their collaborative teams but also refer back to before, during, and after meetings to maintain their focus on the right work.

Major Challenges This Book Resolves

Our experience has taught us that collaborative teams working through the cycle of learning process may experience many distractions and challenges. We have also observed that the schools and teams that are most successful in their collaborative endeavors are those that can inquire into these challenges and then problem-solve to overcome them. These schools and teams understand that while they are implementing each cycle of learning they are also learning how to do the work together better.

Many teams fail to take the first tentative steps on their PLC journey because of their fear of getting things wrong. To assist schools on their journey to becoming a highly effective PLC, we have identified in the final pages of this introduction some of the major challenges with which schools and teams struggle as they attempt to implement the cycle of learning process.

This book is designed to address these common overarching challenges, eliminating the fear that threatens to inhibit progress while also helping teams and schools cultivate a culture where cycles of learning can flourish.

Lack of Clarity

Many teachers get excited about working in a collaborative team, only for that feeling to evaporate as they become overwhelmed or confused when attempting to implement the change process. This is even more pronounced when teams feel unsupported or don't know where to turn for clarity. Though initially energized by the possibility of taking control of their curriculum, owning the assessment process, and meaningfully engaging in discussions about their teaching practice, their progress will often stall because team members don't actually know what to do in their meetings or understand what the outcome of their collaborative endeavors should be. As unfocused efforts fail to affect student learning, the motivation to keep working together ultimately deteriorates into the maintenance of the status quo.

When there is too much ambiguity about the work they should be doing, teams either default to the way they worked previously or spend too much time deliberating on what they *might* do rather than just doing it—all because they are not sure what *doing it* looks like. Busy educators do not have time for lack of clarity to get in the way of improving student learning. The twelve actions and associated tasks outlined in this book are designed to provide teams with the clarity they need.

Inability to Resolve Key Issues

If members have not yet developed a true inquiry mindset, this lack of clarity can become a genuine stumbling block that results in the surfacing of issues that teams often struggle to resolve. The following are some of the most common questions that schools and teams fail to resolve.

- How do we decide which teams need to work collaboratively?
- What if we don't teach the same content?
- How do we get team members to fully commit to the process?
- How do we find a genuine common purpose for meeting?
- What is the work that we need to do?
- How do we make sure we don't just rebadge our meeting as a PLC, in reality doing very little differently than what we've done before?

This last question in particular surfaces over and over again.

We have found that when a school inquires deeper into the actions and work required of their collaborative teams, there is little specific guidance in the PLC literature to give them the information they are looking for. This results in them feeling that, rather than actually changing the nature of their work, their only option is to rename the work they already do. We understand the PLC process needs to be inquiry based, but we also recognize that the ambiguity associated with inquiry prevents teams from taking the key actions and tasks required to impact student learning. Addressing this ambiguity for educators and leaders is central to this book.

Not Understanding the Nature of Inquiry

A genuine inquiry approach doesn't lend itself to the development of an orthodoxy that might guide a team in its work. Any orthodoxy that gives a prescriptive step-by-step description of what a team should do is problematic because it can rob the team of the opportunity to build its own solutions to the problems it is trying to solve. This is why we strongly advocate that team members work on becoming problem solvers, building their individual and collective abilities to inquire through action research into which teaching practices have the greatest impact on student learning.

Lack of a Schoolwide Culture to Support Collaborative Teams

It is important to remember that the success of a collaborative team depends on how the school culture and structures support and nurture its work. This is one of the critical considerations for success that we have observed over the years: schools that have successful, high-performing, and impactful collaborative teams nurture these teams in a schoolwide environment in which purpose and priority are aligned. Where this doesn't occur, the work of collaborative teams can become fragmented, ambiguous, and an exercise in time wasting. As a result, team members can feel disgruntled, disillusioned, overwhelmed, and unmotivated.

Unproductive Team Collaboration

For collaboration to be truly productive and to genuinely affect the learning of both educators and the students they serve, team members must continuously improve their skills and the tools they use as they implement the required collaborative team actions.

Robert J. Marzano, Tammy Heflebower, Jan K. Hoegh, Philip B. Warrick, and Gavin Grift (2016) explain that productive collaboration "should fall into the category of high-depth interactions: discussing research-based instructional strategies, planning lessons, reviewing assessment data, and so on" (p. 25). The nature of these conversations can create what Robert J. Garmston and Bruce M. Wellman (2016) describe as *cognitive conflict*, which can make team members feel uncomfortable. Creating a safe place to navigate this discomfort is key to having substantive conversations among collaborative team members. It is in these conversations that fundamental thinking can be altered in some way. Marzano and his colleagues (2016) see the outcomes of these conversations as second-order change leading to genuine and substantial shifts in the culture and structure of an organization. We argue collaborative teams that are not engaged in this rigorous process are not engaged in the PLC process.

We have observed team after team collapse at this juncture. Excuses such as "We don't have time," "They are just blockers," "We already do this," "You don't know my team," and "That's not my job" become justifications for not genuinely attempting to engage with peers in ways fundamentally different from how they did before. These excuses are often symptoms of collaborative teams not being supported to develop the professional dialogue skills necessary to successfully interrogate their own and others' teaching practices. We also provide additional tips on how collaborative teams can streamline their processes and increase their productivity in appendix A (page 167).

Cultivating a collaborative culture that improves teaching practice on an ongoing basis is central to improving learning outcomes for students (DuFour et al., 2016). In our experience, educators want to spend time collaborating on the work that makes a difference to their teaching practice but are often interrupted in doing so by other initiatives, programs, priorities, and directions that are forced on them from above. The same is true for leadership teams, who often feel the tension between system priorities and the priorities of their individual schools. Clarifying and committing to the right work is the first step in overcoming these challenges.

We wish you well in your collaborative endeavors and hope that this book assists your school's journey to become a high-performing PLC.

SECTION 1
Preparing the Learning

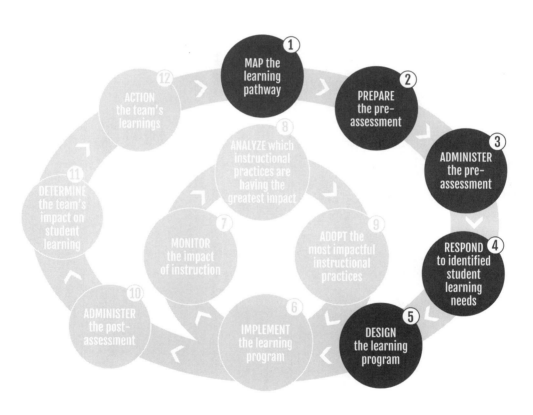

1. MAP the learning pathway
2. PREPARE the pre-assessment
3. ADMINISTER the pre-assessment
4. RESPOND to identified student learning needs
5. DESIGN the learning program
6. IMPLEMENT the learning program
7. MONITOR the impact of instruction
8. ANALYZE which instructional practices are having the greatest impact
9. ADOPT the most impactful instructional practices
10. ADMINISTER the post-assessment
11. DETERMINE the team's impact on student learning
12. ACTION the team's learnings

Action 1
Map the Learning Pathway

At a Meeting

Although standards and curricula are often prioritized in educational documentation, it is the progress toward the standards and meeting curricular goals that is important. This "progress" can be seen as a road map which supports instructional planning.

—Helyn Kim and Esther Care, 2018

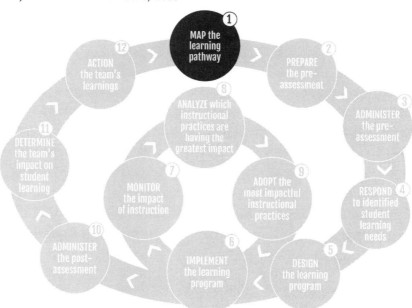

To map the learning pathway, collaborative teams need to have clarity on what it is they want their students to know and be able to do as a consequence of their upcoming cycles of learning. Our experience demonstrates that there is a need for team members delivering the same content to have clarity about what skills and knowledge are *non-negotiable*: skills that all students must acquire as an outcome of the cycle of learning. This ensures that the inconsistent standards of "outcome lotto"—the result of educators relying on their individual understanding and interpretation of the curriculum—are avoided. This first action in the cycle of learning process helps educators to address the first critical question of the PLC at Work process: What do we want our students to learn? (DuFour et al., 2016).

The Tasks

Identify the Skills, Knowledge, and Dispositions (at the Curriculum Level of Proficiency) for the Prioritized Standards

Teams are best supported in taking this step when what Marzano and his colleagues (2016) refer to as a *guaranteed and viable curriculum* has already been identified at the whole-school level. Even in the absence of a guaranteed and viable curriculum, a collaborative team can review the national or state curriculum documents to clearly determine and reach agreement on the skills, knowledge, and dispositions that are the intended outcomes of the upcoming cycle of learning.

Carrying out this task, a collaborative team must first draw on the curriculum to identify the prioritized standards to be addressed through the upcoming cycle of learning. The team should then break these standards down into the specific skills, knowledge, and dispositions that will be the focus of teaching. This is what all team members must then commit to teaching in their classrooms and ensure that students master. The skills, knowledge, and dispositions identified are calibrated directly to the level of proficiency stated in the curriculum documents.

Through collaborative investigation of the curriculum and subsequent discussions and dialogue, all teachers become clearer on the outcomes they require students in their class to achieve in the upcoming cycle of learning. Without this clarity, teachers often go into their classrooms aiming for different levels of proficiency or with different interpretations of what the students must know and be able to do to have achieved the required standard.

Determine the Most Essential Prerequisite Skills and Knowledge as Well as Ways to Enrich and Extend Students Who Have Already Reached Proficiency

Once team members have agreed on what the curriculum standard means, the next task is to determine the necessary prerequisite skills students need to have mastered to be able to successfully learn the at-standard skills. Through these discussions and collaborative endeavors, team members ensure that any essential prerequisites that are pivotal to student achievement are identified and can be incorporated into the teaching program should students need these revised or retaught. In identifying the prerequisites, teams need to be mindful that they don't have the time to reteach all the prerequisites, so only the most essential prerequisites should be included as they map the learning pathway. These prerequisites may need to be taught with a more direct teaching approach than they were previously to ensure that the students can move on in their learning. If some students haven't learned the prerequisite skills in a previous year, it is imperative that they master these as quickly as possible to allow them to engage in the at-standard requirements of this cycle of learning. If we are genuinely trying to close the learning gap, time doesn't allow us the luxury of teaching these skills without a great sense of urgency and priority.

Once a collaborative team has identified and agreed on the essential prerequisites, members can move on to identifying the skills, knowledge, and dispositions that students might progress to during the cycle of learning if they are already proficient in the at-standard skills or reach proficiency before other students in the class. This aspect of mapping the learning pathway allows the collaborative team to consider several options: the team can enrich the learning of these students, extend them into the content of the next level of learning, or choose a combination of both.

We use the term *extend* to mean the deliberate and considered action of moving the proficient student to a higher level of skill and knowledge, which is often drawn from the curriculum for the following year. This needs to be done with careful consideration and thought as it has consequences for the teacher who has the student the following year.

We define *enrich* to mean having proficient students use the at-standard skills, knowledge, and dispositions in some way. This usually involves some application of these proficiencies in tasks or activities, perhaps employing higher-order thinking. This allows for deepening proficient students' understanding and application of their skills, rather than moving them to new content at a higher level. This takes students beyond just skimming the surface.

Often, we miss the opportunity to genuinely enrich the learning of students, failing to create a solid foundation that higher levels of understanding and future content can be built on in our rush to advance them through the curriculum. To be effective, collaborative teams must carefully consider whether they are going to extend or enrich the learning for their students when faced with this choice.

When mapping the learning pathway, we strongly recommend that the documentation created is structured around these three levels: (1) prerequisite level, (2) at-standard level, and (3) enrichment level. We have found that there is no need to list anything in relation to extension. If the decision is made to extend a student into the next year's work for a given cycle of learning, the team (or teacher) can just refer to the learning pathway from the grade level above. For example, consider a third-grade team that is planning for a cycle of learning on the topic of fractions. Despite team members knowing they will need to extend certain students in this topic area, the learning pathway that the team members develop for the grade 3 cycle of learning on fractions doesn't need to include the skills, knowledge, or dispositions related to the equivalent grade 4 cycle of learning. The team should instead access the learning pathway for the fraction topic at the grade 4 level and use this to extend students' learning.

Once all these elements have been determined and agreed on, they can be turned into learning goals or intentions for the individual or series of lessons that make up a cycle of learning. These learning goals can then be converted into *I can* statements so that the learning pathway becomes a student-friendly map that can be shared with and understood by students as they move through the cycle of learning.

Undertake Professional Learning Related to This Cycle to Develop Teachers' Understanding of the Content and Possible Ways to Teach It

Once a team has mapped the learning pathway, the next task is to ensure that all team members are clear on what each learning goal means. If they have developed the learning pathway together, they will already have had rich discussions that will have deepened their understanding. However, if the team is using a learning pathway that another team created in a previous year, it is imperative that team dissects, discusses, and critically evaluates the pathway and its content to ensure clarity for all collaborative team members using the inherited document.

This may require professional learning, which can be carried out in a number of ways. For example, teachers who have previously taught the cycle of learning might share their knowledge about particularly effective modes of delivery with their colleagues. Team members can also do some content-specific research, which might include, for example, looking at textbooks, performing external research, or speaking with other colleagues who have previously taught the content.

Discuss Ways of Sharing or Displaying the Learning Pathway With Students

Another important part of mapping the learning pathway for a cycle of learning is discussing possible ways of sharing and communicating the pathway with students. Simply stated, a learning pathway is really a prioritized and sequenced list of what students will master through a cycle of learning. John Hattie (2012) highlights the importance of making sure that students are clear on the learning goals for each lesson. Sharing goals is becoming a part of many educators' practice (often referred to as *learning goals*, *learning intentions*, or *WALT: We are learning to*), and sometimes these lesson goals are unpacked through the provision of success criteria so that students are aware of what is required to show they have successfully achieved their goals (Clarke, 2001).

While we are strong advocates of sharing success criteria with these practices, students' learning and engagement in their learning are maximized when they are aware of the whole learning pathway—the sequence of learning—they are undertaking. As such, another key task that highly effective teams perform during meetings is discussing the way that the learning pathway will be shared with students. This discussion ensures that this important task is considered by all team members and not left up to the individual.

The way that the learning pathway is shared with students will depend on their age. We have seen many creative teachers of younger students demonstrate learning pathways for their students with interesting classroom displays, such as learning trees with specific skills, knowledge, and dispositions written on each leaf; learning caterpillars, where each segment lists the separate learning goals; and learning rockets, with each stage of the rocket consisting of milestones on the learning pathway. These displays clearly show, usually through the use of colors, which skills are prerequisite skills, which are at-standard skills, and which are related to enrichment work associated with the learning pathway. Sharing the learning pathway with older students might mean displaying an enlarged copy of the learning pathway document the team has created in each classroom. In some schools we have seen students issued with their own smaller version of the learning pathway to add to their workbooks.

Our own observations have confirmed that when students not only know the particular goal of each lesson but also see how these goals fit into the larger sequence of learning, they are able to understand the relevance of the skills and knowledge that they are learning. Brenton Prosser, Bill Lucas, and Alan Reid (2010) found that when students can clearly see the sequence of learning, they are more likely to be able to make connections to past and future learning, increasing their motivation and desire to learn. When the learning pathway is illuminated in this way, students working on the prerequisite skills, for example, understand that they need to master these so that they can move on to the at-standard skills. This can increase student engagement and interest, motivating them in their continued learning success.

Discuss Ways of Communicating the Learning Pathway With Parents and Caregivers

Another aspect of mapping the learning pathway that collaborative teams should consider as they plan for a cycle of learning is how they might communicate this pathway with parents and caregivers. This communication ensures that parents and caregivers are kept informed, are actively involved in understanding the learning process, and have the opportunity to support their child during the upcoming cycle of learning.

We have seen many different ways of communicating this information, including term course outlines, regular learning newsletters, parents' information booklets, and the use of online platforms. The vehicle is less important than the act of ensuring that parents and caregivers understand what children need to master to be deemed proficient. Sharing this information in advance or at the start of each cycle of learning helps to provide a context and deeper understanding of the required level of proficiency.

Implementation Challenges
The School Doesn't Have a Guaranteed and Viable Curriculum

A challenge that can be revealed as the learning pathway is mapped is a lack of agreement regarding the specific skills, knowledge, and dispositions that students must acquire by the conclusion of the cycle of learning. While it can be undertaken by individual collaborative teams as they refer to published curriculum documents, this action is much more focused and targeted when the school has developed a guaranteed and viable curriculum. In this context, *guaranteed* means that the same skills, knowledge, and dispositions are taught in all classrooms of students doing the same course, while *viable* means that these can be taught in the time available to teachers.

Initiating the development of a guaranteed and viable curriculum early in a school's journey to becoming a PLC is the responsibility of school leaders. Requiring vertical and horizontal alignment of the curriculum across the school, the process provides the opportunity for educators to learn from one another and to strengthen their curriculum knowledge. The school and each collaborative team need to be clear on the skills, knowledge, and dispositions most important that students achieve proficiency in for each specific grade level and subject. This ensures that the teachers can then structure learning experiences to focus on the aspects that have been identified as essential during each cycle of learning.

The process of developing a guaranteed and viable curriculum is about prioritizing the most essential skills and knowledge rather than eliminating chunks of the curriculum. Once identified, collaborative teams must focus their unwavering attention on these essential aspects through each cycle of learning to ensure that they are actually mastered to the standard required. The other skills detailed in the curriculum should still be taught but not with the same degree of collaborative focus as the aspects deemed to form the guaranteed and viable curriculum.

In the process of developing a guaranteed and viable curriculum, it is imperative that school leaders provide the communication channels necessary for horizontal and vertical alignment to ensure gaps and overlaps are avoided. Our experience has shown us that educators constantly articulate that they are time poor, whether they are leaders or teachers. While they cannot create more time, school leaders can prioritize the development of their school's guaranteed and viable curriculum over other administrative or technical tasks.

Providing all educators with a clear explanation of why a guaranteed and viable curriculum is crucial to the work of a highly effective and learning-focused PLC is vital. Having been developed strategically, the rationale for each element of this curriculum must also be explained clearly. If educators can see how the development of the curriculum assists their collaborative team, they will also be able to see the time spent on this task as an important investment in supporting them and the work they do to achieve high levels of learning for all. School leaders need to develop a clear implementation plan or pacing guide that outlines the major steps in their school's PLC journey. This needs to be communicated to all staff so that they understand what aspect of the PLC process is being undertaken at any given time, what resources and time will be available, and the expected time frame for associated tasks to be carried out. If a school does not yet have a guaranteed and viable curriculum, this pacing guide must include time for its development.

One of the challenges that we have seen many schools experience is their leaders failing to see the PLC process as whole-school transformation, instead viewing it exclusively as the work of collaborative teams and pushing the development of a guaranteed and viable curriculum into team meeting time. This challenge can be avoided by leaders ensuring that sufficient time outside of team meetings—for example, a series of staff meetings or pupil-free days—is devoted to the development of their school's guaranteed and viable curriculum early in the process of becoming a PLC. By working on its development outside collaborative team meeting times, team members can genuinely focus on implementing the cycle of learning process that we advocate for in this book during their meeting times.

The development of a guaranteed and viable curriculum cannot be outsourced to a curriculum leader, a curriculum team, or even a group of committed teachers. Rather, all educators at a school must be involved to ensure the success of the process. We have witnessed firsthand what is possible when schools embrace and commit to the process as a whole-school undertaking and provide the time needed to do it. The rigorous discussions, debate, and ultimate agreement that can be reached in these settings support educators to deepen and extend their individual and collective knowledge of the state or national curriculum that they have the responsibility of implementing.

High levels of learning for all students can't be achieved unless there are corresponding high levels of learning for all educators. Clarifying exactly what students need to be proficient in is a vital and compulsory component of any school's journey to become a high-functioning and learning-oriented PLC. Mapping the learning pathway for each cycle of learning is supported, enhanced, and simplified when the school has created a meaningful guaranteed and viable curriculum for its students. Developing a guaranteed and viable curriculum is not an event but an ongoing process. Each cycle of learning offers school leaders the opportunity to monitor and, where necessary, make adjustments to their school's curriculum based on the feedback from collaborative teams as they learn by doing.

The Team Never Seems to Reach Agreement on What They Want Students to Learn

Sometimes differences of opinion can get in the way of schools and collaborative teams agreeing on what a priority standard is or what the essential learnings embedded in the priority standard are. These differences of opinion can arise for many reasons. For example, when teachers have been teaching in a particular subject area for a long time, they might develop the belief that they have an exceptional understanding of the content and, on the basis of this belief, strongly advocate for the status quo to be maintained. Their familiarity with the subject may cause them to ignore or discount other factors that might be used to determine a curriculum standard's importance. Sometimes these educators might feel threatened because they think that if things change, they will not be able to teach something that they've always taught and like to teach. It is important that decisions aren't made based on what people want personally but instead are made on the basis of what is most important for students' learning.

All staff should have had rigorous discussions and reached consensus about the learning priorities for their subject and grade level when developing a guaranteed and viable curriculum. If this process has been undertaken with a spirit of genuine inquiry, educators will have already clarified the most important skills and knowledge within the curriculum. So, when collaboratively mapping out the learning pathway for an upcoming cycle of learning, a great deal of time should not be needed to determine the most essential learnings. Discussion should instead focus on ensuring all team members interpret the prioritized standards in the same way and with the same level of rigor.

It is the job of educators to raise concerns, advocate for their ideas, and provide their professional opinions during the process of developing a guaranteed and viable curriculum. However, once it has been developed, it is the team's responsibility to accept the decisions and develop learning pathways from its school's curriculum with integrity, knowing it will have the opportunity to provide feedback as a part of the cycle of learning process.

The use of discussion protocols provides a way for team discussions to allow different points of views to be aired and, ultimately, team consensus to be reached and a decision to be made. As collaborative teams use these protocols and become more familiar with working as a problem-solving team, differences of opinion will be embraced as a way of providing the team with a variety of options to consider and explore. Teams unfamiliar with productive conflict may find differences of opinion uncomfortable or see them as getting in the way of their work, rather than accept it as a way of deepening the quality of their work and enhancing their understanding of how they can construct learning experiences for their students.

Once teams have aired differing points of view, considered the merits of each, reached consensus, and made a decision, all with the support of structured protocols, it is important that they then move on to the subsequent actions in the cycle of learning—more specifically, how they will teach the essential knowledge, skills, and dispositions to ensure all students reach the level of proficiency required. In essence, everyone must commit to a decision once it has been made, regardless of how they feel about it, and move on.

One Teacher (or a Few) Dominates the Collaborative Process

Another challenge that collaborative teams need to be conscious of is not always deferring to a teacher who has taught the content for a long period of time. Such teachers' voices and experiences are important, and their opinions on how to teach the content are invaluable. However, in collaborative team meetings, all team members' voices should hold equal weight.

The purpose of collaborative team meetings is for educators to form ideas together. As such, it is important that all team members understand the true nature of collaboration. When one voice dominates, particularly that of a more experienced teacher, other team members may feel that they must always defer to that person's experience. More experienced teachers may also assume that it is their job to lead less experienced staff in this way. However, in a high-performing collaborative team, a teacher with a high level of content knowledge and particularly impactful teaching skills serves as a valuable resource for his or her team, and this person's skills are drawn on to support the collective commitments his or her team makes. Such teachers use their knowledge and wisdom gained by experience to support their colleagues' learning, rather than just tell team members what to do. While there will be occasions when teams become stuck and genuinely need the direction of more experienced teachers, a high-performing collaborative team does not allow this to become the default way of working.

The actual words used to describe the structure of collaborative teams can reinforce a perception of hierarchy. Often collaborative teams will have a nominated leader, and in many schools, this is the most experienced teacher on the team. The actual title *leader* can convey a hierarchical arrangement of authority and, consciously or subconsciously, impress on members that this person's opinions are more important than others' opinions. High-performing teams are those in which the nominated leader is indistinguishable at meetings from other team members. This person acts more as a facilitator of the meeting processes and discussions, guiding the team in a manner that doesn't imply authority or superiority. The voice of this person doesn't dominate, nor does his or her opinion override and curtail the individual thinking of team members or the collective problem-solving focus of the team.

Team Members Differ in Their Commitment to Communicating the Learning Pathway

Collaborative team members having varying beliefs and opinions about the value of involving students or parents in understanding the learning pathway can be problematic. For example, some team members might believe that their job is done when they have taught the content, regardless of whether the students have learned it or not. These beliefs can jeopardize a team's commitment to tasks related not only to this action—mapping the learning pathway—but also to subsequent actions.

Once educators within a team understand what is required for students to know and be able to do to be proficient, it becomes important to discuss ways in which this can be communicated to students as well as parents so that there can be genuine and extensive opportunities to celebrate learning growth through each cycle of learning. However, we have observed that some team members believe it is not really necessary to share the learning pathway and that it is just another task on their long list of things to do.

Communicating the learning pathway to students and parents provides the basis for the celebration of student learning growth. By ensuring that both students and parents are aware of the expected learning pathway, celebrations of student learning, explained further in subsequent actions, can be more genuine and better understood. This is because educators will be able to demonstrate to students and their parents and caregivers the progress they have made along the learning pathway, rather than just present what the student achieved.

Sharing the learning pathway contributes positively to students knowing what it is they are meant to be learning, increases their engagement and motivation to learn, and assists them to see that learning is nested in levels of complexity. Collaborative teams cannot allow team members' differing beliefs to undermine the important task of communicating the learning pathway, or any other aspect of the cycle of learning process.

Team Members Just Want to Plan Activities

Few teachers would argue that teaching isn't a complex and daunting task, or that there is anything more stressful than feeling inadequately prepared with learning activities to keep students occupied. While it is important for teachers to have activities planned for their students to complete, this feeling can sometimes lead teachers to just plan or source activities only vaguely related to prioritized standards or the specific needs of their students. Often, the desire is to move too quickly to considering what they will get their students to do, resulting in activity or lesson planning becoming the primary work of the collaborative team. As experienced teachers, we fully understand the impulse to default to this option to avoid the stress of feeling underprepared. Given how time-poor teachers are, we also fully understand why the focus of many collaborative teams is just that.

Even in the initial stages of each cycle of learning, it is imperative that teams do not rush through or pay lip service to the process. The development of learning experiences and learning activities is fundamental; however, the skills, knowledge, and dispositions must first be understood, and all team members need clarity on the level of rigor and proficiency required for students to be deemed at standard. This clarity will ensure that the activities and learning experiences subsequently developed by the team in later stages of the cycle of learning process are strongly aligned and support student achievement.

The School Wants to Adopt Another School's Guaranteed and Viable Curriculum

There is a temptation for schools to adopt the guaranteed and viable curriculum of another school. We understand this a very seductive prospect, given how time-poor schools and educators are, but in the long run this is counterproductive to the PLC process. It actually robs educators of the opportunity to deepen their curriculum knowledge, compromising team members' depth of understanding and ability to map the learning pathway because they haven't had the opportunity to engage in the rich discussions involved in developing their own curriculum.

Without this level of discussion, team members assume that all educators have the same understanding of what it is they are about to teach. These assumptions can lead to teachers in different classes implementing the same cycle of learning but aiming for different learning outcomes and levels of proficiency in their students. As a result, the collective responsibility for student learning that underpins the work of the collaborative team is weakened. When team members later start to discuss student learning results, their discussions have already been compromised.

One way that school leaders can ensure this doesn't happen is by giving adequate time to the development of the guaranteed and viable curriculum. We often see collaborative teams trying to develop their curriculum on the run as they attempt to complete the other tasks in preparation for the upcoming cycle of learning, which can lead to cutting corners. When school leaders instead take responsibility for the process of developing a guaranteed and viable curriculum and prioritize making time for educators to work on this important task, the desire and tendency to merely adopt another school's curriculum is minimized, if not eliminated.

We have yet to meet an educator whose curriculum knowledge hasn't been extended and developed by working collaboratively with his or her colleagues to determine the prioritized standards for the students they serve.

The Curriculum Is Overcrowded

This challenge is based on the belief that all elements of the curriculum are equally important and must be delivered to all students. The systems, schools, and collaborative teams that work on this assumption primarily have a focus on *teaching* (delivering content) over a genuine focus on *learning* (students learning what educators are teaching). When there is too much for students to learn, the default response is to churn through the content as quickly as possible to get through it all in the hope that it will stick for some students. As there isn't time to ensure all students learn to the level of proficiency required, the goal becomes just getting through it.

As we've mentioned, developing a guaranteed and viable curriculum is more complex than merely throwing out chunks of the curriculum. It is a systematic, whole-school process of prioritization, followed by monitoring the impact that teaching has on students' learning. Other content and skills of the curriculum will still be taught as they have always been taught, but it is the prioritized standards that will be taught with more urgency and monitored more closely through each cycle of learning. Every effort will be made to ensure all students learn these and achieve the required level of proficiency in the skills, knowledge, and dispositions determined as being essential. As part of a school's commitment to ensuring students reach required levels of proficiency, appropriate interventions must be implemented when students fail to meet necessary standards.

Many systems, schools, and educators feel immense pressure regarding the curriculum and the need to treat the published curriculum as their guaranteed and viable curriculum. But a school's journey to become a PLC—and the work of teams within a PLC—will be compromised if educators continue to feel forced to choose a focus on teaching (just delivering the content) over a genuine focus on students learning the content they deliver.

This challenge is best addressed by courageous school leaders who make sure that educators at their school are clear on the expectations regarding curriculum and support them in developing and implementing their school's guaranteed and viable curriculum. This sets teams up for success in their efforts to map the learning pathway.

Action 2
Prepare the Preassessment

Teaching in the dark is questionable practice.

—Deborah Taba and Deborah Elkins, 1966, p. 23

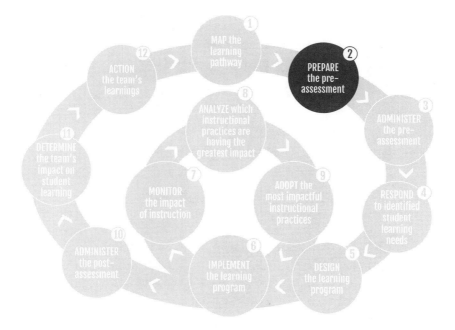

This action requires teams to begin the process of developing their knowledge of what their students' current levels of understanding are with regard to the prioritized standards unpacked in Action 1. It allows teams to address the critical question, How will we know our students are learning? (DuFour et al., 2016) by providing baseline data with which to measure student learning growth and the impact of their teaching practice.

The Tasks

Review Current Learning Data That Relate to This Cycle or Develop Common Formative Preassessment If No Relevant Data Exist

Teams start to carry out this action by reviewing any current learning data that relate to the specific skills, knowledge, and dispositions of the cycle of learning they are about to teach. If no current data relevant to this cycle of learning exist, then collaborative teams need to develop a common formative assessment—typically referred to as *preassessment*—to determine their students' current levels of proficiency.

The term *common formative assessment* is prevalent in the literature on PLCs. To clarify what we mean by this term, we offer the following three points.

1. It is *common* because team members agree on the type of assessment that they will give students before either developing a new assessment or refining or adopting an existing assessment together. The chosen assessment is also implemented in a common way across all classrooms.

2. It is *formative* because it informs:
    -   Students of the next steps in their learning
    -   Team members of individual student learning needs
    -   Team members of common student weaknesses
    -   Team members of the key issues they need to discuss in relation to their teaching practice

3. It is an *assessment* because it is a tool for measurement.

Through the process of developing and agreeing on a common formative assessment, particular attention must be placed on ensuring the assessment includes measurement of students' current levels of proficiency of the skills, knowledge, and dispositions detailed in the learning pathway. The agreed assessment must allow information to be gathered about individual students', classes', and cohorts' levels of proficiency across three levels of performance. With this is mind, the common formative preassessment must be able to measure three levels of performance.

1. Below the learning goal (prerequisite skills)
2. At the learning goal (skills at the required standard)
3. Beyond the learning goal (skills above the required standard)

To save time and to ensure collaborative teams don't become overwhelmed by the sheer volume of their work, it is important to look at what current data exist and what current assessments could be used for this cycle of learning. For example, there might be student learning data from assessment administered in the previous year that could be used to gauge students' current levels of proficiency. These data could become the starting point for the team's investigation into which data are still current and which might need further corroboration. Trust in the reliability of existing data sets is critical to the decisions collaborative teams make regarding whether to use the data or not. As teams become more productive, efficient, and effective in working through the cycle of learning processes, this sense of trust in the resulting data will increase.

A preassessment should also be developed if no reliable or current data exist that can provide team members with clarity regarding their students' current levels of proficiency. Depending on the existence, comprehensiveness, and reliability of any data that are available, this may require the development of a new complete assessment, or it may comprise specific items designed to fill gaps in existing learning data.

One of the benefits of working through this task is that teachers develop a shared and deeper understanding of what being proficient means. Put another way, as they develop assessment tools to determine their students' learning realities, teams become increasingly clear on what being at standard means in their upcoming cycle of learning.

Ideally, this task and the others associated with this action should be carried out two to four weeks before the cycle of learning begins, providing teams with plenty of time to consider and discuss the implications of the results they collect.

While the construction of the items to be included in the preassessment is important to the process, this can happen outside of team meetings. This responsibility might be delegated to team members or taken on by the team leader. What is more critical is the discussion to reach agreement on the assessment tasks and items the team will use. This discussion further builds the team's ability to understand both the content that members will teach and the most effective ways of measuring whether students have learned it or not.

One way that team members can strengthen assessment is by completing the assessment task themselves prior to administering it to their students. This allows them to check the quality of items, address any ambiguities in wording, correct any misalignment of the assessment type with what is being assessed, and discuss and agree on the expected answers.

Discuss the Way the Assessment Will Be Implemented in Each Classroom So That the Data Are Valid and Comparable

Collaborative teams also need consensus on the way that the common formative assessment will be implemented. This is critical to ensure that the collected data are fair, valid, and reliable. There is no general rule about the type of assessment teams should use at this stage of a cycle of learning. It might be performance based, diagnostic, a work sample, selected response, or any other type of assessment, but the choice must be guided by what is required for that cycle of learning. The team should discuss and agree on the conditions for the assessment, including the duration, any resources that students might have access to, teacher directions and support available, and the time of day that it will be administered.

Identify Ways That the Data Will Be Collated So That They Can Be Compared and Analyzed

Clarification and team agreement regarding the way the resulting data will be gathered, how they will be presented, what technology might assist with the process, and the required timelines are critical. If team members are clear on these decisions, this work can be completed outside of team meeting time, allowing the team to instead focus on collaborative analysis and integration of the gathered data in meetings.

Develop the Common Summative Assessment to Be Administered at the End of the Cycle (This Might Be the Same as the Preassessment)

Finally, teams need to consider and plan the postassessment that will be implemented toward the end of the learning cycle. One of the purposes of a cycle of learning is to gauge the individual and collective impact that a team's instructional practices have on student learning. As such, the preassessment and postassessment are integral to the work of the collaborative team as each cycle of learning is implemented.

There are three critical considerations in designing appropriate and complementary assessment to be carried out at the start and end of a cycle of learning.

1. The preassessment must provide an accurate measure of students' current levels of understanding in the skills, knowledge, and dispositions to be taught.

2. The postassessment must provide an accurate measure of the students' acquired levels of understanding in the skills, knowledge, and dispositions that were taught.

3. Both preassessment and postassessment must minimize the likelihood of students simply learning how to pass the assessment (as opposed to truly learning the necessary skills, knowledge, and dispositions).

Depending on the skills, knowledge, and dispositions that are the focus of the learning cycle, the postassessment content may be the same or similar to the preassessment, or the team might develop different assessment content to gauge the level of student learning as a consequence of the cycle. For example, assessment content might be the same or very similar when the cycle of learning is centered on students' ability to recall number facts, while mastery of a particular writing technique would likely be better assessed by requiring students to respond to different prompts at the start and end of the cycle of learning. Though the content of the assessment may be different, it is important for the reliability and validity of the data collected that the *design* of the preassessment and postassessment is the same.

Implementation Challenges

The Team Doesn't Take Into Account What Students Already Know

There is often a tension between educators' understanding of the skills, knowledge, and dispositions they want students to acquire in a cycle of learning and how they then go about supporting students to achieve these. This tension can become a challenge when some teachers, or sometimes collaborative teams as a whole, treat students as empty vessels to be filled with content. By not taking into account what students already know, these teachers and teams ignore the need to provide appropriate differentiated instruction based on specific identified learning needs.

In the absence of an understanding of students' prior knowledge and current levels of proficiency, a teacher in this situation typically delivers the *same* content in the *same* way to the *whole* class. This teacher perceives his or her role as the deliverer of content, rather than as someone who is responsible for finding out what students already know and can do so that he or she can adjust the learning program to meet precise needs.

This highlights the fundamental difference between teachers and teams that focus on teaching (delivering content) and those that focus on learning. It is an alluring and attractive proposition to teach in the same way to a whole class because it is easier, quicker, and more efficient than having to think, act, and build on students' prior knowledge in the specific areas being targeted through a cycle of learning. However, it remains essential that teachers take the time to first understand where their students are in their learning and then tailor learning experiences to ensure high levels of learning for all.

The Assessment—and the Resulting Data— Isn't Fair, Valid, and Reliable

Collaborative teams need to be aware of each member's understanding of effective assessment design. A lack of or incomplete understanding plays out in three specific ways: (1) misalignment between the prioritized skills and knowledge and how proficiency is measured; (2) assessment design that is inappropriate for or unrelated to the focus of the cycle of learning; and (3) an overreliance on tests as opposed to thoughtfully designed assessment.

Teams spend a considerable amount of time developing the learning pathway, but when it comes to assessment development, there can be a misalignment between the prioritized skills, knowledge, and dispositions and what the designed assessment items actually measure. For example, a collaborative team might need to measure students' ability to count by twos but unintentionally develop an assessment item that doesn't actually do that. To avoid this, teams must consciously check that the assessment items match the identified skills and knowledge to ensure a misalignment doesn't occur.

Another challenge occurs when specific assessment design does not relate effectively to the discipline area that is the focus of the cycle of learning. For example, a team may choose a process-based assessment when it would be more appropriate and effective to design a product-based assessment. Teams must build their collaborative capacity to design fair, valid, and reliable assessments by clarifying together what they want students to know and understand. High-performing collaborative teams learn by doing as they develop their assessment techniques and build their assessment literacy over time.

Many teams have a propensity to carry out all assessments as tests. This is evident in schools where the common discourse centers around including a pretest and posttest in learning cycles. It is important to remember that tests are just one type of assessment design at a team's disposal. The word *test* can encumber the process as it implies the reason educators give students an assessment is purely to find out what they know or have learned. Interestingly, the root of the word *test* is *testari*, from Latin, meaning "bear witness" (Testari, n.d.). In comparison, the root of *assess* is *assidere*, also from Latin, meaning "to sit beside" (Assess, n.d.). This highlights a critical difference in our use of assessment design in collaborative teams. When only one type of assessment design, such as tests, is used, it can impact negatively on student engagement and the validity of results. To overcome this, school leaders must monitor each collaborative team's capabilities in assessment design and provide professional learning opportunities to continually build and strengthen assessment practices.

Teams Rely on Commercially Produced Assessments

A common and seductive practice for many collaborative teams is the use of commercial assessments such as those produced by publishing and assessment companies. However, this practice can impede the team's inquiry process.

When collaborative teams use commercially produced assessment tools, the majority of which are in the form of diagnostic tests, they often don't specifically align with the learning pathway identified by the team. This misalignment renders the data gathered from these assessments flawed at best and irrelevant at worst. While there are time-saving benefits, it also robs the team of the chance to deepen and enrich its members' understanding of the content they are about to teach. Externally designed assessments can be a quick and efficient solution to a team's assessment planning, but they are ultimately highly ineffective in supporting educator learning and have little impact in developing team members' individual and collective understanding of the skills, knowledge, and dispositions they want their students to learn.

High-impact collaborative teams know how to use commercially produced assessment effectively and judiciously. They ensure there is congruence between the cycle of learning's focus and the assessment items before they choose this option. They will also design their own assessment items and add them to the assessment of an external provider to ensure that the information gathered matches the learning pathway specifically and addresses any gaps.

In each cycle of learning, team members need clarity on what they will ultimately teach, what evidence will show that their students are learning, and what this means for the way that they will structure learning experiences. When educators fail to understand this and take seductive shortcuts, they create more difficulties and uncertainties and reduce their opportunities to learn with and from their colleagues.

Teams Lack Time to Create Assessments

Lack of time is the perennial issue for schools and staff everywhere. Collaborative teams often identify this as the root of many of the challenges they face, and, in many instances, it is true. Teams that don't meet for at least one hour each week can't possibly carry out the actions outlined in this book and will ultimately need to compromise the process to fit tasks into their agendas. Teams in this position will also focus primarily on getting tasks done as quickly as possible, rather than seeing the purpose for each task.

It is critical that school leaders understand the importance of collaborative team meeting time and structure the timetable in such a way that allows for teams to meet regularly and frequently. Where this occurs, team members are able to collaborate meaningfully, authentically, and productively on the right work. For example, having sufficient time promotes opportunities for team members to engage in essential collaborative tasks, such as deciding on the most effective common assessment, agreeing on its design and implementation, and identifying the most appropriate methods for collating the data they will gather.

This action in the cycle of learning is critical to identify what teaching practices are going to serve students and teachers best, as these decisions will be made based on the resulting data. When time is not provided, is not adequate, or is used unproductively, the opportunity for improving both student learning and teaching practice is compromised. Schools can't create more hours in a day, but they can repurpose the time they have to focus on the actions that have the greatest impact on student and teacher learning.

School leaders are also well placed to be aware of the impact a whole-school assessment schedule can have on the collaborative team process. When top-down assessments are set, school leaders need to ensure they don't compromise the collaborative work of teams, particularly each team's localized emphasis on formative assessment.

In highly effective PLCs, we have seen a reduction in assessments being imposed on teams, with greater emphasis placed on collaborative team–designed common assessments that support current cycles of learning. This enables educators to respond more immediately to student learning needs, supporting the fundamental mission of achieving high levels of learning for all.

Assessment Practices Aren't Common

Educators often ask us early in their adoption of the cycle of learning process, "Why does everyone in our team have to assess the same way?" They express a preference for particular assessment design or methods that they have perceived as successful in the past. The answer is that when teachers don't assess using the same design and agree on creating the same conditions for implementing those assessments, it is impossible to collect data that will allow comparison of student learning from classroom to classroom. This in turn makes all discussions about the impact of the team members' individual and collective teaching practices, subsequent pacing of the team's curriculum, and future collaborative decision making impossible.

DuFour et al.'s (2016) PLC at Work process embraces the notion of a simultaneously loose and tight culture. Creating and implementing common assessments doesn't take away teachers' autonomy to use other formative assessment approaches in their own classrooms on a regular basis. Effective teachers will constantly be checking whether their students are learning what they are teaching. The information they gather allows them to adjust their teaching practice accordingly and explore ways of teaching things differently when they are not getting the results they want. Nothing in this action or the associated tasks robs teachers of that opportunity. Using team-developed common assessments ensures the data that teams use is fair, valid, and reliable, and can be compared. It promotes genuine collective responsibility for all the students the collaborative team serves, not only those who individual teachers are directly responsible for in their own classrooms.

Action 3
Administer the Preassessment

At its best, preassessment can turn on the lights. It can illuminate student thinking, interests, learning preferences, experiences and even the content itself. Armed with the most current classroom-level data about student understanding and skills, teachers can make proactive, timely decisions about the instruction that will enable learners to achieve mastery.

—Jessica A. Hockett and Kristina J. Doubet, 2013, p. 54

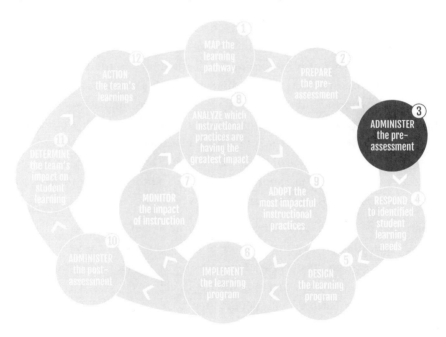

The third action in the cycle of learning process is administering the preassessment. Rather than being implemented at a collaborative team meeting, this action is carried out by the team members in their individual classrooms.

The Tasks

Administer the Preassessment

The preassessment planned in Action 2 (page 25) needs to be administered in classrooms well in advance of the implementation of the actual cycle of learning, unless the team already has relevant learning data specific to what will be taught. This allows collaborative teams the time to respond to the resulting learning data, which provides information on the individual and collective needs of the students in their class and the cohort as a whole.

The expectation is that teachers correct and score their students' preassessments and collate the data using the agreed process in their own time. By completing these tasks outside of meetings, team members maximize the available collaborative time for discussions that focus on the implications of the data they gather to inform the planning of the upcoming cycle of learning.

When implementing this action, it is important for teachers to consider how they communicate the purpose of the preassessment with their students. By making sure students have a clear understanding of this, teachers support the development of a strong learning culture in their classroom. While the way this is communicated will be guided by the age of the students, it is important for all students to understand that the preassessment allows their teacher, and teachers of students in other classes, to support their learning by working out where they are on the learning pathway. In addition, students need to understand that the information collected from the preassessment is used to ensure that the learning needs of individuals, groups, and the whole class can be addressed. Depending on the age of the students, it may be beneficial to let the students know that they will also get the opportunity to reflect on their own results so that they understand their next steps on the learning pathway.

Students may be used to only being assessed at the end of a sequence of learning, so in the initial stages of implementing the cycle of learning process, it is very important to reassure them and explain the purpose of the assessment. This includes noting that there will be aspects of the assessment that they will not be able to do, and that this is expected because this what their teachers will support them to learn across the cycle of learning.

By having an accurate understanding of their students' current realities, team members are then able to move into discussing what actions teachers need to take to address students' learning needs.

Action 4
Respond to Identified Student Learning Needs

Data are not information; information is that which results from the interpretation of data.

—Ian I. Mitroff and Francisco Sagasti, 1973, p. 123

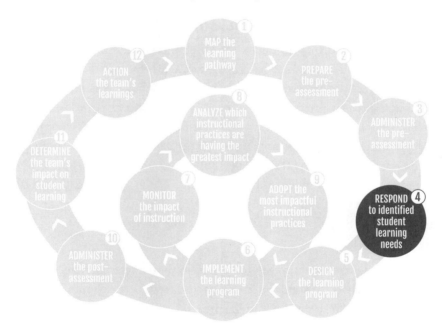

This critical action in the cycle of learning process is carried out at a collaborative team meeting when members have collated the assessment data and are ready for presentation and analysis. In completing this action, team members do the work to ensure they are able to address the third and fourth critical PLC questions: How will we respond when some students do not learn? and How will we extend the learning for students who are already proficient? (DuFour et al., 2016).

The Tasks

Discuss the Results of the Preassessment or the Other Data Being Used to Determine Students' Current Level of Understanding

The first task in this action involves teams engaging in rigorous discussions about the results of the preassessment and any other learning data that they have previously agreed to use. Reviewing this data should allow the team to determine the needs of the cohort and individual students, including whether there are any specific prerequisite skills that need to be revised or retaught before moving on to teaching the at-standard skills and knowledge. From the data, the team should be able to determine what might need a more intensive focus, the areas of common misunderstanding, and which students need to have their learning enriched or extended. For example, if the learning data reveals the majority of students in a cohort are struggling with some of the prerequisite skills, the most urgent focus for the team would become ensuring that students master these quickly during the early stages of the cycle of learning.

Develop a Pacing Guide for the Cycle of Learning

It is imperative that teams conduct a thorough interrogation of the learning data because the more detailed their analyses are, the more targeted and focused the plan they create to address the learning issues that they identify will be. The point, which can't be stressed enough, is to ensure that the team actually uses and responds to the learning data they have gathered to pace out how the learning cycle fits into the number of lessons available for its implementation. While many teams implement preassessments, often the data are only used to establish a baseline so that student learning growth can be measured at the end of the sequence of teaching. While the data gathered through preassessment do serve this important purpose, they should also be used to determine the pacing of the teaching program so that the learning needs of students can be specifically targeted and addressed.

In the development of this pacing guide, the team should reference any whole-school scope and sequence charts or similar documents that indicate its school's yearly curriculum implementation plan. As a result of the preassessment, the collaborative team will have up-to-date data it can use to determine how many weeks the learning may actually require. Willingness to adjust previous plans based on learning data is a key aspect of a PLC's unrelenting focus on learning rather than just the delivery of content.

It is important to note that collaborative teams will only be able to fully plan the earlier lessons in the cycle of learning at this stage of the process. As more learning data are collected throughout the cycle of learning, the focus of later lessons in the pacing guide can be confirmed.

Drawing From Professional Learning and Research, Discuss the Instructional Strategies and Teaching Practices That Can Be Used to Make Teaching as Strong as Possible

Another key task for collaborative team members preparing for a cycle of learning is identifying and discussing the possible instructional strategies and teaching practices that they can use to ensure students master the skills and knowledge that the preassessment has shown must be the initial priority for student learning. It is through these discussions that collaborative teams maintain and strengthen their focus on learning.

In their discussions of instructional strategies and teaching practices, team members must aim to identify the approaches that will have the greatest impact on student learning and will ensure that their teaching practice is as strong as it can possibly be from the very start of the learning cycle. The team will have had some preliminary discussions of possible instructional approaches and teaching practices during earlier phases of the cycle. Now, using learning data that more clearly identify the learning needs of their specific students and classes, the team can confirm which of the previously discussed instructional approaches and teaching practices that members will use.

As they discuss the most appropriate instructional strategies and teaching approaches to support the highest level of learning for students, teachers may need to undertake professional learning or conduct research to increase their teaching repertoire and knowledge. For example, the preassessment a team carries out might indicate that the whole cohort is lacking several prerequisite skills. Understanding that they aren't able to dedicate as much instructional time as they might like to teaching these skills without compromising on the time they will need to teach the at-standard skills, team members might recognize a need to use more explicit instruction techniques. The team would need to check that all members clearly understand what explicit instruction is. Some team members might perceive explicit teaching as being more about gradual release of responsibility, whereas other teachers might see it as just showing or telling the students how to do something. To ensure that it is used with fidelity, the strategy must be clarified through collaborative team discussion, and some members may also need to engage in further research to strengthen their understanding of the agreed instructional practice.

As mentioned previously, one of the key purposes of a collaborative team meeting is to be the forum for job-embedded professional learning wherein educators learn from their colleagues and through collaborative research. This is an important part of the cycle of learning and is embedded into many of the actions collaborative teams undertake.

Develop a Team SMART Goal Based on the Current Level of Proficiency of Students in the Cohort

The nature of the goals developed by a PLC is based on the work of Jan O'Neill and Anne Conzemius (2006). The use of *SMART goals*—goals that are strategic and specific, measurable, attainable, results oriented, and time bound—in a PLC is deliberate as they ensure a school avoids creating goals that may sound impressive but fail to provide any real direction or impact in improving student learning. In addition to ensuring an unrelenting focus on improving student learning, the use of SMART goals supports the development of a school's orientation toward results and ensures that evaluation of staff's collaborative efforts is based on tangible facts and evidence rather than mere perception or hopeful thinking.

Once teachers have clarified the sequence of learning, developed the pacing guide, and identified the possible instructional strategies that they might use, they are ready to develop a SMART goal for their upcoming cycle of learning. This SMART goal should be expressed as a percentage of student proficiency to be achieved by the end of the cycle of learning, based on the cohort's starting level of proficiency determined through the preassessment.

The importance of the SMART goal for each cycle of learning can't be underestimated. It is the glue that binds the work of each member of the collaborative team. SMART goals provide clear targets that team members work individually and collectively toward achieving by the end of each cycle of learning.

Implementation Challenges

Teachers Don't Follow Agreed Common Assessment Practices

Even after the collaborative team discussions in which consensus has been reached, team members sometimes bring back flawed and unreliable assessment data for analysis. In some cases, after continued probing, it becomes clear that teachers haven't followed through with their commitment to implement common assessment in the way agreed to as a team. This means that the resulting data aren't fair, valid, and reliable. This compromises their team's discussions and ability to plan from an accurate understanding of the current learning needs of the students in their class and in the cohort.

A wide variation in the learning data brought back to the collaborative team meeting can indicate that a team member did not implement the agreed method or score in the same way. The validity of the data gathered through the preassessment needs to be monitored closely, and, where large variation occurs, the cause must be investigated. This careful and mindful monitoring will determine whether the variation is an accurate reflection of ability across individual classes or an indication that team-agreed actions regarding assessment implementation haven't been adhered to outside the meeting.

Teachers Become Defensive When Discussing Assessment Data

When teams are just starting to use the cycle of learning process or members don't have high levels of relational trust, educators can be suspicious that their learning data will be used by others to judge their skill as a teacher. This belief may cause them to be hesitant, cautious, and even defensive when sharing or discussing the learning data pertaining to their students and classes.

Another reason that teachers may be hesitant to disclose or discuss the learning data of students in their class is because they feel the information gathered doesn't match the inherent knowledge, understanding, or abilities of their students. Before the cycle of learning even commences, these team members often feel compelled to justify the results rather than look at the current reality presented by the learning data. In such instances, they typically do not, or are reluctant to, participate in discussions of the learning data, hampering their team's endeavors to address student learning needs that should otherwise surface.

In implementing this action and associated tasks, the data being discussed must be drawn from the preassessment or any other agreed data set. It is important that team members understand that the purpose of collecting and bringing the learning data back for team discussion is for their collaborative team to be able to identify and cater for the range of skills and knowledge of students in their classes and across the whole cohort more adequately. It is also worthwhile for team members to acknowledge that feeling judged is a normal part of the process and that many of their colleagues may be feeling the same way. This stage of the cycle of learning provides the perfect opportunity for team members to practice their data-analysis skills and to reinforce the ways they will use learning data in subsequent phases of the learning cycle, building and strengthening relational trust within their team.

A Teacher Doesn't Bring His or Her Data to a Meeting

When collaborative teams start the cycle of learning, one of the obvious pitfalls is that teachers might not have the learning data ready by the agreed timeline. This may be caused by a number of factors. For example, it may be that the teachers did not schedule it into their program to ensure that they had implemented the assessment prior to the agreed meeting. No matter the reason, the result is that precious meeting time is wasted because the team can't move forward in its discussions. Further to this, any discussions they do have will lead to a flawed pacing guide due to an incomplete data set.

An underlying cause of this might be that such a team member is not truly committed to the process itself and, either consciously or subconsciously, sabotages the process. Not adhering to team decisions and agreed actions has implications for team norms and how breaches are addressed. It also has implications for the way the school leaders and team leaders respond to such breaches as they bring all team members aboard their school's PLC journey, a key aspect of which is to take collective responsibility for the learning of all students.

Team norms are very important, and teams should establish norms that deal with noncompliance. In high-performing collaborative teams, issues of nonadherence to team agreements will have been anticipated in advance with a clearly developed process to address any instances that may arise. Given the impact on the functioning of the team, instances of nonadherence must be addressed expediently and in a professional manner.

A simple mantra of a highly effective PLC is "Unprofessional behaviors that are not challenged are accepted." One of the keys to success is pre-empting any issues that might arise by developing and agreeing on processes that allow team members to challenge noncompliance in a respectful and professional manner.

Teachers Disagree on the Need for a Pacing Guide

A lack of agreement on the need for a pacing guide often stems from teachers' fear of losing autonomy in their classrooms. In the cycle of learning process, there are key milestones and tasks that team members need to commit to. All team members must be prepared, with agreed tasks completed, so they can have rich discussions and make appropriate decisions to improve student learning.

It is important that teachers understand the need for having a common learning pacing guide. The aim of a pacing guide isn't to synchronize the delivery of every activity or dismiss a teacher's unique teaching personality but rather to ensure that the key tasks that need to be done are done. Because of their impact on the work of the collaborative team, these tasks must be scheduled into the program of every member.

Developing an agreed pacing guide as a team ensures that the collaborative process is set up for success and ensures that team members maintain a focus on working collaboratively rather than as independent, isolated contractors.

Time Is Wasted in Meetings

Working collaboratively requires discipline and a high level of skill. We know how time-poor educators are, but teams often waste valuable time in meetings talking about perceptions and opinions rather than focusing their discussions tightly on what the data are telling them and what they are committing to in response to ensure high levels of learning for all students. This generally shows that the team is not using a protocol or a series of governing questions to frame discussions.

The use of discussion protocols allows teams to structure their discussions in a way that makes them increasingly focused and targeted. In this particular action, this practice ensures that the discussion first centers on the validity of the assessment data and then on determining the actions that team members will commit to take to address the areas of need they identify.

A SMART Goal Is Not Developed for Each Cycle of Learning

Challenges arise when collaborative teams don't set a SMART goal for the upcoming cycle of learning or instead set a very general goal that doesn't specifically state the level of student achievement being aimed for. We have also seen teams play it safe by setting goals that do not challenge members to change the status quo or that reinforce the belief that their efforts have little impact on student learning.

Skipping the development of a SMART goal has further implications because it denies the team a clear, specific target that unites its members in collective responsibility for improving student learning. We define a *collaborative team* to be a group of people working interdependently to achieve a goal that they couldn't achieve by working in isolation. If a team doesn't have a goal that members work collaboratively to achieve, it isn't really a team by definition—instead, it is just a group. High-performing collaborative teams see the development of SMART goals as a serious undertaking and use them to identify their collective endeavors and gauge their ultimate success. These teams celebrate when they achieve or exceed the goal they have set and take it personally when they do not.

Teams will often default to writing goals as they always have. As a result, the goals they write may not meet the SMART structure. To overcome this, it is important that school leaders support teams to understand what a true SMART goal is and develop their skills in setting them. A well-written SMART goal for a cycle of learning might be recorded as follows:

> By the end of week six of this term, 85 percent of students will be at or above the at-standard level in the skills, knowledge, and dispositions that have been the focus of this cycle of learning as determined by the postassessment.

We have often observed goals that are more general, revolving around the implementation of activities or the delivery of a certain program rather than being explicitly tied to improvements in student learning and levels of proficiency. However, the creation of a student learning–focused SMART goal is an absolutely essential component of each cycle of learning because it demonstrates to team members whether they are able to move on to the next cycle of learning.

School leadership can misstep when they impose SMART goals on teams. Collaborative teams need to develop and own their own SMART goal directly related to their current cycle of learning. In addition, collaborative teams need to be able to see how their short-term SMART goal complements longer-term SMART goals that may have been set by school leaders. Team-developed SMART goals are the smaller steps toward the achievement of their school's annual SMART goals. In many high-performing PLCs, school leaders collect each collaborative team's SMART goals and results at the end of each cycle of learning as a way of tracking progress toward their school's annual goals.

The Same SMART Goal Is Set for Each Cycle of Learning

Some teams have a standard SMART goal target for each cycle of learning that doesn't change as they move through different cycles. However, it is important that each cycle's SMART goal is based on the current reality of the cohort of students as determined by analyzing data collected through preassessment. To do this, team members must examine the data on a deeper level and have rigorous discussions about what they want the outcome of their teaching to be.

By adjusting the SMART goal for each cycle of learning, team members guarantee that the goal is set at a level that is attainable and is seen by team members as being realistic. If the team does not perceive the SMART goal as attainable, members will not take the necessary actions in their classrooms to actually try to achieve the stated level of proficiency.

SMART goals are the glue that binds a team together in its collaborative endeavors. A genuine and purposeful SMART goal is one that inspires team members in their individual and collective endeavors to achieve high levels of learning for all. It builds and supports the interdependence of team members as they work together to achieve the goal they have set.

Action 5
Design the Learning Program

At a Meeting

In high performance learning cultures, teachers are inquisitive, increasingly knowledgeable and well informed about becoming better practitioners together.

—Andy Hargreaves and Michael Fullan, 2012, p. 127

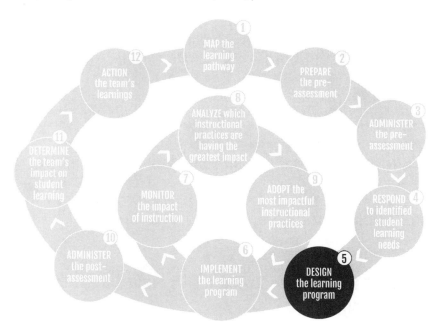

We know that collaboration that centers purely on administrative tasks, the sharing of resources, and activity planning has no real positive effect on student learning and achievement (Jensen, Hunter, Sonnemann, & Cooper, 2014). With this in mind, and having completed the preceding actions and associated tasks, teams must ensure in this action that their collaborative endeavors in designing the learning program make the greatest possible impact on student learning. This will then be monitored and modified in forthcoming actions. When completing this action, team members must also explore ways of catering to the diverse learning needs of their students, allowing their collective endeavors to be guided by the third and fourth critical PLC questions: How will we respond when some students do not learn? and How will we extend the learning for students who are already proficient? (DuFour et al., 2016).

The Tasks

Develop Engaging Learning Activities That Clearly Relate to the Skills and Knowledge That the Team Wants Students to Learn

Designing the learning program requires team members to source and develop engaging learning activities that motivate students to learn and are targeted directly at their students' individual and collective learning needs. At this point of the collaborative process, teachers must drill down into their teaching practice and what their instruction is actually going to entail in relation to the identified learning pathway and the specific learning needs of their students.

In many schools, particularly those with less of a learning focus than their PLC counterparts, teachers design their learning program without the knowledge gained through implementing the previous actions in the cycle of learning process. Often, designing the learning program becomes their sole, though flawed, collaborative endeavor.

As a consequence of having carried out the previous actions, team members will have a greater understanding of the learning pathway, have clarified what their students already know and don't know in relation to the intended learning, and have explored possible teaching strategies and approaches that research suggests might benefit student learning. At this point in the process, collaborative teams are in the best position to plan strategies, programs, and activities based on what students need and not just on personal preference or what was implemented in a previous year.

Plan for Other Ways to Extend and Enrich Students Not Requiring Explicit Teaching

An important aspect of this part of the process is making sure team members discuss how they plan to cater for students who have demonstrated they have already reached proficiency or are likely to do so very quickly. In designing the learning program, teams develop learning activities that require students to go beyond what is actually taught in class so that they can make inferences that lead to new understandings. At this point in the process, teams can also consider what Marzano and his colleagues (2016) refer to as *knowledge utilization*. This requires students to apply knowledge learned in specific situations and in particular ways in novel situations using different ways of thinking.

Thinking taxonomies can be very useful to teams when considering the challenge of extending and enriching learning for students. Importantly, these taxonomies should refer to levels of thinking that increase in complexity and sophistication as you move through them. Different ways of thinking inherent in many taxonomies are cognitive processes such as recalling, defining, describing, comparing, inferring, sequencing, speculating, imagining, evaluating, and hypothesizing. Or, as mentioned earlier, if you feel you cannot enrich a student's knowledge any further despite moving through a thinking taxonomy, you may choose to move the student on to a related cycle of learning from the next grade level.

Essentially, this task specifically focuses teams on addressing the fourth critical question of the PLC at Work process: How will we extend the learning for students who are already proficient? (DuFour et al., 2016). By doing so, teams can develop learning programs that engage all students through cycles of learning, not just those who need greater intervention to reach proficiency.

Develop Common Quick Checks to Closely Monitor Student Learning

The research validating the role that formative assessment plays in achieving higher levels of learning is unequivocal. The use of formative assessment techniques to change teaching practice in particular is supported by the pioneering and foundational research of Paul Black and Dylan Wiliam (1998). Quick checks are a practical way of implementing formative assessment practices. Also referred to as *unobtrusive formative assessment strategies*, quick checks enable teachers to collect information on the impact of the actions being trialed during the cycle of learning (Marzano, Warrick, Rains, & DuFour, 2018).

Designing the learning pathway also provides teams with the opportunity to consider what common quick checks they will implement to closely monitor the learning progress of their students. We use the term *quick checks* to refer to formative assessments that do not take a long time to administer, relate to the specific learning goals that are the focus of instruction, and enable collaborative teams to analyze the progress of learning within a cycle. They are short, sharp, and focused assessment tools that allow individual teachers and teams to monitor student learning in a timely manner so that teaching practice can be adjusted immediately to maximize this learning. Examples of quick checks include the following.

- Exit slips (students record key learning from the lesson before leaving class)
- Sticky-note tracking (students place a sticky note on one of three categories: I got it, I need to clarify, or I need small-group instruction)
- Classroom polling (students respond to key questions—verbal or written—from their teacher designed to ascertain their different levels of understanding)

- Criteria checkers (students and teachers check off elements of learning goals that indicate how they are progressing in their understanding)
- Card cluster (each student writes one key understanding on a card, which is then grouped with other students' cards to create a visual display of levels of understanding)

Many schools are familiar with pre- and postassessment regimes. We feel this approach alone is flawed as it doesn't allow educators to quickly determine the impact of their instructional approaches during the teaching and learning process or enable them to adjust their teaching practice as they implement learning programs. The exclusive use of pre- and postassessment regimes seems to be more about measuring student learning growth than providing a way for teachers to adjust their teaching practice immediately when students are not learning.

By collaboratively designing and agreeing on when and how to implement common quick checks, teams will gain fair and reliable evidence of student learning on which to base their collective decision making during the cycle of learning. Rather than having data to discuss only at the end of the cycle, by carrying out this task, teams have access to ongoing and relevant data that allow them to monitor their impact on student learning and make necessary adjustments to their teaching practice immediately.

Implementation Challenges
Learning Activities and Learning Goals Are Misaligned

The impact of the learning program can be restricted at this point in the cycle of learning as a result of misalignment between the skills, knowledge, and dispositions a team has decided are essential and the planned activities. This is usually caused by teachers selecting activities they have always done, regardless of their congruence to the specific learning goals, or selecting activities solely because they are fun and engaging rather than supportive of the achievement of the learning goals. Teams can increase the impact of their teaching and corresponding levels of student learning when they select activities that align with the agreed learning goals. Teachers may still select ideas and activities they have previously used, but they must base these decisions on the way they support and strengthen student learning rather than just their personal preference.

Effective collaborative teams draw from a wide range of resources to design their learning programs. Grounding their decisions in the prioritized skills and knowledge, they elevate learning above their personal preferences and avoid making selections based on ease or convenience.

As teams become familiar with working through a cycle of learning, they can use activities and strategies that proved successful when they implemented similar units of work in previous years to strengthen the learning program. Documenting successful practices and activities, and filing everything in an orderly and organized manner, can assist future teams in designing their own learning programs in years to come. Rather than starting from scratch, new collaborative teams will have strong foundations on which to build their learning programs.

Collaborative team members who ask themselves the wrong questions in team meetings can also run the risk of ending up with misalignment between the learning program they design and its intended outcomes. Questions we often hear that indicate a focus on activities rather than learning include the following.

- What do we need to do?
- What do the students need to do?
- What are we going to do for the first four weeks?

When these are replaced with questions that focus on learning, teachers can guarantee greater congruence between what they want students to learn and how they intend to teach it. For example, consider the following.

- What are the specific strategies, activities, or programs that will help students to achieve the learning goals we want them to achieve through this cycle of learning?
- As we look at what students already know, what might the first four weeks of this cycle of learning look like?

Teams Overplan

Planning too many activities compounds the problem of limited instructional time. When time is limited and a team has too much to get through, the tendency is for teachers to churn through content and see completion as the ultimate goal, rather than focusing on student learning and proficiency.

Teaching is not just keeping students busy but ensuring that whatever it is that teams design supports the learning that they seek.

Teams Don't See the Importance of Ongoing Formative Assessment

The genuine lack of understanding of the purpose of common quick checks throughout a cycle of learning can create obstacles for collaborative teams. Quick checks enable teams to swiftly determine whether their individual or collective teaching practices are having the desired impact on student learning. Without them, teams are "flying blind."

This affects their ability to determine which teaching approaches are proving to be the most beneficial in supporting student learning, ultimately preventing other team members from implementing successful strategies in their classrooms during the same cycle of learning.

Quick checks are designed to be quick. They shouldn't take up too much instructional time in the classroom or, in the analysis of data, at the collaborative team meeting. Quick checks also don't need to be applied across a whole cohort. For example, a team might collect work samples from a group of students being closely monitoring based on what has been identified from preassessment data. A team might also use quick checks to monitor a group of students identified as requiring specific support when developing its SMART goal.

It is important to note that while teams develop and plan the implementation of common quick checks, individual teachers must still continue to monitor student learning progress in their individual classrooms. Teachers shouldn't misconstrue the purpose of common quick checks. They are specifically designed to help the collaborative team make instructional decisions about what teaching practices and approaches are working and which are not. They are not a justification for reducing the strategies teachers use individually in their own classrooms to check for understanding. It is vital that both common quick checks and individual teacher quick checks are used consistently and not at the expense of the other. High-quality teachers always check in, find out where students are, adjust the teaching practices being used, support their students in different ways, and guide them through the learning pathway.

To ensure common quick checks don't contribute to the belief of not having enough time, it is important that teams carefully consider the design of these unobtrusive assessments (Marzano et al., 2016). For example, a thirty-question multiple-choice quiz is less likely to be a true quick check than an exit slip that asks students three pertinent questions as they exit their lesson. The skilled use of quick checks can reduce the need for more complex and time-consuming assessment approaches. Collaborative planning of common formative assessment is critical for ensuring teams have an ongoing and manageable plan for monitoring their impact on student learning.

SECTION 2
Implementing the Learning

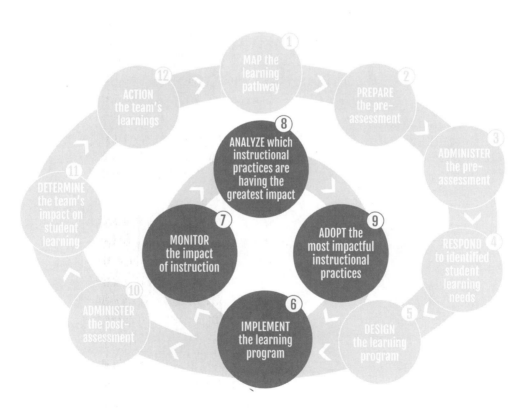

Action 6
Implement the Learning Program

The best teachers are not always, not even usually, those teachers with the most sophisticated content knowledge. The best teachers do know their material, but they also know a lot about the process. They have at their disposal a repertoire of instructional methods, strategies, and approaches—a repertoire they continually cultivate, just as they develop content knowledge. They never underestimate the power of the process to determine student learning outcomes.

—Maryellen Weimer, 2008

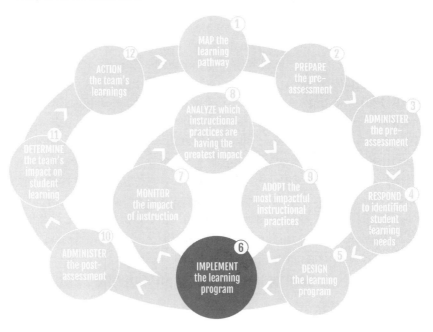

Action 6 is where the cycle of learning process moves from preparing to doing. This action requires teachers to commit to implementing what they have collectively agreed is the best course of action in their classrooms. Through the previous actions, teams will have carefully and deliberately considered the curriculum, the practices conducive to highly impactful teaching, the specific needs of their students, and the learning activities they will implement to ensure these needs are met. Individual teachers must now

51

implement the agreed learning program and common assessments, making informed adjustments to their teaching practice to ensure that all students achieve high levels of learning as they move through the cycle of learning.

The Tasks

Share the Preassessment or Appropriate Learning Data With Students and Have Them Set Specific Personal Learning Goals

In the earlier phases of the cycle of learning, collaborative teams determined the current level of proficiency of their students through the preassessment or other appropriate learning data. In the classroom, teachers can now share this learning data with the whole class or individual students so that they understand clearly what they already know, how this relates to the cycle of learning, and what they still need to learn to reach proficiency as a consequence of the learning program. In some highly effective and learning-focused classrooms, we have also observed teachers sharing their team's cycle of learning SMART goal with their classes as a way of motivating and challenging them in the learning they then undertake together.

Referring to the learning pathway, students can at this point set specific individual learning goals appropriate to their own level of learning. These specific learning goals aim to progress students from where they are at the beginning of the cycle to where they need to be at the end. By knowing the progression through the cycle of learning, students are able to become more active participants in the learning process and see the relevance of the learning experiences they will undertake to the goals that they set. This goal setting will be approached differently at different stages of schooling, taking into account the maturity level of students. For example, in a lower-elementary school setting, a teacher may confer with his or her students, explaining what they have already mastered related to the cycle of learning and suggesting possible appropriate learning goals to set. As they become familiar with the process of goal setting and increase in maturity, students become more capable of setting their own learning goals.

Explicitly Teach the Identified Skills and Knowledge Related to the Cycle of Learning

Teachers now have the opportunity to explicitly teach the content, adjusting the learning experiences they planned in the previous phase of the learning cycle to ensure that they suit the individual learning needs of students in their classrooms. They must use their professional judgment and intimate knowledge of their students' learning needs to determine which elements of the cycle of learning might be best learned through whole-class instructional sessions and which need to be covered through smaller teacher focus groups in which they can target the specific needs of particular groups or individual students.

When students have established their own learning goals, they begin to understand more fully the purpose of the whole-class instruction they receive and see their involvement in teacher focus groups or intervention sessions as a support to them in the achievement of their goals, rather than as a punishment for nonlearning.

At this phase of the learning cycle, teachers should differentiate the structures they use in the implementation of their teaching program to ensure that students achieve the learning goals they have set. The success and impact of these organizational arrangements and student groupings must be continually informed by the common quick checks developed in Action 5.

Organize Teacher Focus Groups and Student Groupings Based on the Preassessment Data (and Subsequent Quick Checks)

As teachers reflect on the learning of their students, they must continually adjust their teaching approach, the pace of their teaching, and the groupings of their students to ensure that all students' learning needs are being addressed during the cycle of learning. In this situation, nonlearning is not seen as a reflection of a student's ability but rather as evidence for the teacher that his or her teaching strategies or classroom grouping structures need to be adjusted to ensure all students reach the required level of proficiency.

Teachers implementing a cycle of learning might simply structure student groups within their own individual classrooms; however, depending on timetabling constraints, teams may also choose to bring students with similar learning needs together in flexible, short-term groups across the whole cohort so that they can receive intensive instruction at their immediate point of learning.

In education there is a movement toward personalizing learning for students, but this can mean many different things to different educators. At this phase of the learning cycle, teachers are in the position to personalize the learning approaches they implement in their classrooms—the teaching strategies they use and the way they structure learning experiences. Differing amounts of instructional time, diverse teaching approaches, and varying intensities of intervention support must be provided to ensure that all students achieve at high levels.

Implement Ways to Extend and Enrich Students Not Requiring Explicit Teaching

In their own classrooms, teachers are continually looking for opportunities and ways to extend or enrich the learning of students not requiring explicit teaching. At this point in the cycle of learning, teachers can implement the learning program that allows these students to build on and enhance their knowledge and understanding. If planned effectively, this will assist students to apply their knowledge and understanding in real and practical ways without just providing them with more of the same or automatically moving them on to content of a subsequent grade level.

Implementation Challenges

Teachers Don't Follow What's Set Out in the Pacing Guide

Even though their team will have worked collaboratively to plan the cycle of learning, when teachers return to their own classrooms, they do not always implement the plan with fidelity. While we strongly encourage teachers to modify and adjust their teaching practices and organizational structures to meet the needs of the students in their classes, collaborative teams should monitor these adjustments closely. Individual teachers and the collaborative team need to ensure that modifications and adjustments made in the classroom don't compromise the process or affect the team's collective responsibility for all students learning at high levels.

One of the key non-negotiables in the cycle of learning process is that teachers must deliver the key content in their individual classrooms as set out in their pacing guide. Without this alignment, it becomes impossible to bring common learning data back to the meeting in a timely fashion. This then compromises a team's ability to have rich discussions about the learning progress of its cohort and specific groups of students. If teachers are at different points of the cycle of learning in their individual classrooms, it also means their team can't interrogate the data to determine which teaching strategies are proving to have the greatest impact on student learning.

Teachers must be able to respond to the specific learning needs of students in their own classes; however, team members need to know that certain set points are non-negotiable and must commit to them for the cycle of learning process to have the impact on student learning that we know it can.

Students Don't Learn in the Time Allocated

The opposite and equally problematic challenge is collaborative teams becoming so reliant on structure that they do not modify their pacing guide, even if it is clear that their students are not reaching the required level of proficiency.

For example, a collaborative team might have determined in its pacing guide that by the end of the second week of implementation it wants all students to be proficient in three specific skills. When members analyze the common quick check data, however, they find that in all classes the students' levels of achievement are still well below standard. At this point, team members should discuss the issue and make a collaborative decision about what they will do. It is likely that the team would decide to alter the pacing guide to extend the amount of time allocated to teach these skills.

The very reason we refer to a team's plan as a *pacing guide* is that the term *guide* implies that collaboratively agreed adjustments can be made to the plan based on evidence of student learning. This ensures that teams maintain a focus on learning rather than merely delivering content to students and moving on, whether students have learned it or not, just because the allocated time has run out.

Changes to the pacing guide should only be made after discussion and negotiation between all team members. Collaborative teams should see themselves as problem-solving teams in the truest sense. When students do not learn in the time frame initially set out, teams must take responsibility and adjust their pacing to ensure that they meet the learning needs of all students. If individual teachers note that students in their classes aren't progressing with their learning in the way the team anticipated when developing the pacing guide, they should bring up the matter at a team meeting so that all team members can problem-solve and make a collaborative decision about what action needs to be taken.

Student Groupings Can't Occur Across Classrooms

We have observed that the way students are grouped can become an excuse for not engaging in the cycle of learning process. In some instances, educators adopt the belief that students need to be grouped across all the classes undertaking a specific cycle of learning. If their timetables don't allow this to occur, they choose not to undertake this work.

While we have seen teams implement this cohortwide approach successfully, this organizational arrangement is dependent on many variables in a school and is not the only way to meet disparate learning needs. The process can also be implemented effectively within individual classrooms.

The organization of student groupings should be given careful consideration to ensure that it provides learning experiences appropriate to the needs of each individual, based on the learning pathway set out in the current learning cycle. Teachers often fear a loss of autonomy in the cycle of learning process; however, within their individual classrooms, teachers actually have a great deal of autonomy in terms of how they group their students to meet their individual needs.

Grouping students within each individual classroom can be the most appropriate way for some collaborative teams to meet their students' learning needs, but it can also be a starting point for more complex groupings. As teams see the positive impact of directly addressing the needs of homogenous groups of students, they can then choose to pursue other grouping options, including ways of extending these groupings across multiple classrooms.

No matter what structures are put in place for grouping students, it is imperative that these groupings are short term, targeted, flexible, and designed to ensure that students can quickly move on to the at-standard level of work. We have often seen students locked into groups that become a form of streaming or tracking. These groups, rather than being designed to serve the needs of students, trap students on a certain learning trajectory, denying them access to the at-standard content.

The formation and adjustment of student groups must be informed specifically by the feedback teachers receive from quick checks, observations, or other assessment techniques. The aim for the teacher of any student in a lower-achieving group is to close the gaps in his or her learning and get the student out of that group as soon as possible.

Action 7
Monitor the Impact of Instruction

In the Classroom

The careful monitoring of student progress is shown in the literature to be one of the major factors differentiating effective schools and teachers from ineffective ones. Indeed, those analyses which have sought to determine the relative effect sizes of different instructional practices have identified monitoring student progress as a strong predictor of student achievement.

—Kathleen Cotton, 1988, p. 1

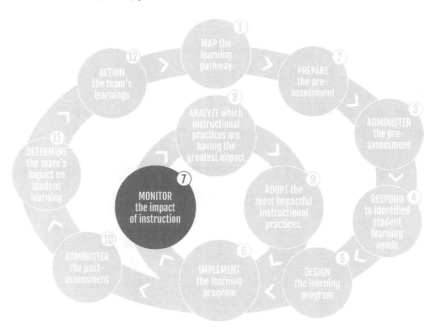

Monitoring the impact of what they do and adjusting their practice accordingly are the linchpins of teachers' professional growth. It requires the use of ongoing evidence of student learning and incorporates both student and teacher in the collecting and monitoring of that evidence. Celebration becomes the catalyst to support continued learning for both students and teachers. When both students and teachers recognize the results of their efforts, it reinforces the belief that they can be—and are—highly successful learners.

The Tasks

Carry Out Frequent Quick Checks to Continually Ascertain Students' Levels of Learning in the Targeted Skills and Knowledge

As teachers explicitly teach the content identified by their collaborative team, they must continue to carry out frequent quick checks. Regardless of whether these quick checks are designed by the team or individual teachers, they are crucial. Quick checks allow teachers to adjust their teaching approach immediately and respond at the point of need.

Provide Continual Feedback to Students on Their Learning Progress

Teachers can use the results of these quick checks to continually provide feedback to students, enabling them to see where they are positioned on the learning pathway. This helps students understand learning as a process and develop self-motivation as they monitor their own progress toward achieving their personal learning goals. Provided with feedback on their learning growth and depth of understanding, they will be able to see the progress they have made. Students' involvement in the learning process also helps them to view the teacher-student relationship as a partnership.

As Gavin Grift and Clare Major (2020) outline, an important aspect of this feedback loop is that it also gives students the opportunity to provide feedback to their teachers. This includes students articulating the things that a teacher may be doing that support their learning as well as where they are having difficulty.

Have Students Continue to Monitor and Record Their Learning Progress, and Review and Revise Their Personal Learning Goals

This feedback loop allows students to continue to monitor and record their own progress toward achieving their specific learning goals. Through ongoing monitoring and revision, teachers ensure students continue to set further relevant goals and build their awareness and understanding of the progress they are making in their learning. Demonstrating that through continued effort they can and will improve their learning, this goal-setting process supports students to develop a growth mindset.

One of the most effective ways of monitoring and recording the progression of learning is through the use of student portfolios, sometimes referred to as *learning logs*. In this approach, teachers encourage students to do the following.

1. Track and record their understanding against the learning goals set out in the learning pathway.

2. Determine whether or not they've met the learning goals using criteria checklists, bar graphs, or other visual means of recording teacher feedback, assessment results, and self-reflections.

3. Set new learning goals if the evidence shows they have achieved their initial goals.

4. Act on feedback on how they can improve if they have not met their learning goals.

Celebrate Student Learning Growth

As they focus relentlessly on high levels of learning for all and motivate their students to continue learning even when they hit obstacles, it is absolutely vital that teachers celebrate learning growth. Continually recognizing and celebrating student learning growth develops a genuine culture of learning in which growth takes precedence over the grade or mark achieved.

Whether the evidence for learning growth comes from individual conferences, peer assessments, or quick checks, it is important that time is built into the class program to celebrate. By acknowledging the small steps each student makes toward achieving his or her learning goals, the focus on learning is strengthened. This reinforces the notion that, even though they may be at different stages along the learning pathway, all students can learn.

There are many ways we have seen collaborative teams and classroom teachers celebrate student learning growth. These include the following.

- Displaying individual students' achievements in the classroom with visual representations such as data walls and classroom achievement thermometers

- Acknowledging achievements verbally through conversations with students

- Presenting certificates of accomplishment

- Giving out peer-recognition awards assigned by students

It is important to recognize that sometimes these celebrations may need to be private, while at other times they can be more public whole-class or group celebrations. Sensitivity to individual student preference in this regard and paying attention to the way learning progress is discussed in class has two main benefits.

1. Students are able to view the process as a positive celebration of learning, an experience that contributes to the ongoing development of self-efficacy.

2. Students are less likely to compare themselves to other students, which can reduce self-efficacy and slow their progress toward the achievement of a required standard.

To do this effectively, teachers need to understand the individual dispositions, personalities, and key motivators of their students, ensuring that the approaches they take to celebrating student learning are appropriate and positive and build a true learning culture. Just as highly effective teachers individualize their teaching approaches for students in their classrooms, they also consciously consider how to rationalize the celebration of their students' learning growth.

Implementation Challenges

The Feedback Doesn't Inform Instruction

Teachers often underestimate the power and impact of feedback, viewing it purely as a mechanism for providing information to students. Monitoring the impact of instruction, however, promotes formative feedback wherein students also share information with their teachers, enabling them to better assist with their learning. The more opportunities educators give students to share what they are thinking, the more targeted their assistance and support can be.

Any feedback received from common or individual quick checks is designed to be used by teachers to inform their instruction. However, when quick checks are used only to assign a score, they are not formative because teachers don't then make instructional adjustments to improve student learning in response.

Data from common quick checks also allow individual team members to formulate new ideas with their colleagues by calling on their team's collective wisdom. For example, an individual teacher might have identified some students in his or her class who are taking a long time to develop an understanding of something deemed essential. When team members explore what can be done to support the learning of these students, they become a true problem-solving team, and with collective inquiry they can often suggest a range of approaches that the teacher might adopt to address his or her challenge. This arms teachers with a range of options and minimizes the risk of defaulting to the more traditional response of reteaching the content slower and louder.

Students Aren't Meaningfully Involved in the Assessment Process

Another challenge that can surface during this phase of the cycle of learning is in the assessment process itself. When teachers don't triangulate the sources of assessment, they might not be getting the full picture. Information needs to be collected from three sources: (1) the teacher, (2) the peer, and (3) the students themselves. Information that teams and teachers collect may include student work samples, results from common quick checks, peer reviews, self-reflections, student-annotated assessments (where students are given the chance to explain their thinking on an assessment after it has been marked), and co-constructed rubrics where applicable.

We are strong advocates for allowing students to develop partnerships with teachers in their learning journeys. The most effective teachers work hard in cycles of learning to help students understand the important role they play in their own learning and the genuine voice they have in the learning process. As a result, students see learning not as something that is done to them but as something they actively engage in. This promotes persistence and resilience when it comes to learning. Further, students come to understand that the learning process itself is also dependent on what they bring to the experience. This includes the thinking habits they need to develop and the attitudes they need to apply to be successful learners. The outcome is that they become less reliant on their teacher as the sole support for their learning. This constructive approach to learning requires teachers to find ways to encourage students to make meaning from their own learning experiences and become actively involved as a true partner and participant in their own learning journey.

Student Learning Progress Isn't Celebrated

Educators get so busy that they often forget to prioritize time to celebrate student learning growth. In a PLC, educators are consumed by a desire to progress all students toward or beyond the expected standard. Celebrating small gains as students work their way through each cycle of learning motivates and compels them to continue on their learning journey.

Collaborative teams and teachers celebrate student learning growth by talking about it, bringing it out in the open, visualizing what it looks like, recognizing specific things that contribute to growth, capturing and discussing different ways of thinking about growth with students, and building these celebrations into the structure of their lessons and routines. Celebration of student learning growth should be seen not as something that happens only at the end of a cycle of learning, but as something that is part of the daily practice of all educators as they go about their work.

Without celebrations, learning can become disengaging and sterile. Hard work and persistence can give way to mediocrity and a lack of student engagement when there is no "fruit" for the labor exerted. Students can feel they are on a never-ending treadmill and become exhausted by the process if they receive no genuine acknowledgment of the small learning steps they make along the learning pathway.

Action 8
Analyze Which Instructional Practices Are Having the Greatest Impact

The most important factor affecting student learning is the teacher. In addition, the results show wide variation in effectiveness among teachers. The immediate and clear implication of this finding is that seemingly more can be done to improve education by improving the effectiveness of teachers than by any other single factor. Effective teachers appear to be effective with students of all achievement levels, regardless of the level of heterogeneity in their classrooms.

—William L. Sanders, S. Paul Wright, and Sandra Patricia Horn, 1997, p. 63

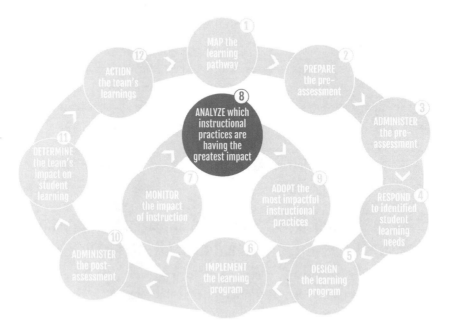

Action research comes to the fore in this phase of the cycle of learning process. Each cycle of learning allows teams to investigate the strength of their instructional approaches while they are implementing the learning program. By doing this on an ongoing basis, collaborative team discussions can focus on analyzing the instructional practices being used in individual classrooms. Using common quick checks to collect data on the impact of their teaching on student learning, team members are able to collaboratively identify teaching strategies and practices that have the greatest impact on student learning and those that do not. As teams complete this action and its associated tasks, members engage in job-embedded professional learning with their colleagues, researching the strength of their individual and collective teaching practices.

The Tasks

Identify and Celebrate Successful Teaching Practices and Identify Less Successful Teaching Practices With Common Quick Checks

If the other actions in the cycle of learning have been carried out with fidelity, teams should have fair, valid, and reliable data with which to not only check student learning but also determine which teaching practices used by team members have the greatest impact on student learning.

At this phase of the process, the link between teaching practice and student learning is emphasized. This can be uncomfortable for teachers, but it is important nonetheless. Our experience has taught us that high levels of learning can only be achieved with quality teaching. Therefore, the only way to improve student learning is to push through this discomfort to improve teaching quality.

Teachers who have had the greatest impact on student learning should have the opportunity to celebrate their achievements and, most importantly, fully explain their approaches to their colleagues. Teams may consider other ways of learning more about the teaching practices that are having the greatest impact rather than just having successful teachers explain their methods. For example, a team might decide that observing the practice of a particularly impactful teacher might help members better understand the nuances of this teacher's approach.

Discuss How Teaching Practices Can Be Adjusted So That the Most Impactful Strategies Are Implemented in All Classrooms

As collaborative teams identify, discuss, and learn about the teaching practices having the greatest impact on student learning, the expectation should be that teachers not using these approaches incorporate them into their own teaching repertoire and abandon those that have proven to be less impactful. The central aim of the cycle of learning process is to continually enhance teaching practice so that students in all classrooms benefit from what their teachers are learning about the practices that have the greatest impact on student learning.

At this point, the focus of team discussions and meetings shifts from What is it that we want students to learn? to What teaching practices are most impactful in helping students learn what we want them to learn? Collaborative teams must then explore how all members might adopt or adapt these successful practices so that all students benefit.

Check on Progress Toward Achieving the Team's SMART Goal

The data that are collected through common quick checks also allow collaborative teams to check on their progress toward achieving the SMART goal that they would have set at the beginning of the cycle of learning. We strongly advise collaborative teams not to wait until the postassessment at the end of the cycle of learning to do this. Each of the common quick checks that team members implement in their classrooms provide data that form snapshots of how a team is advancing toward achieving its SMART goal.

Ongoing monitoring of their progress allows a team to make midcourse adjustments to their pacing guide based on what they discover. For example, as the result of checking on its progress toward achieving its SMART goal, a team can determine which skills and knowledge need more instructional time, which have been learned fully and can be moved on from, and which have been learned only superficially and might need to be the focus of intervention sessions for refinement.

Implementation Challenges

Teams Don't Centre Their Discussion on the Effectiveness of Their Practice

As teams carry out this action and the associated tasks, it is imperative that discussions don't focus superficially on an analysis of the learning program or activities. Rather, teams are required to thoroughly analyze and interrogate the teaching practices being employed to implement the learning program and activities. The core purpose of working collaboratively in the cycle of learning process is to enhance the individual and collective instructional competence of team members by increasing teachers' understanding of the strength of their own teaching practice.

High-performing collaborative teams are open about the way they teach, discussing their teaching practice freely with one another to continually develop the strength of their practice so that they can improve the learning outcomes of the students they serve. This can only happen if team members commit to openly discussing what they implement and, most importantly, how they implement it.

Some teams find this action challenging and, rather than having open and honest discussions, they create excuses, ignoring the connection between what teachers do and the level of student learning. As emphasized previously, collaborative teams must understand that they are involved in action research to determine how to best teach the identified skills, knowledge, and dispositions so that all students reach proficiency. Using the learning data to understand the impact of their teaching practices, identifying those that have the greatest impact on student learning, and learning about them collaboratively so that they can apply the most effective practices in their own classrooms must become the obsession of all team members.

The key is that the collaborative team meeting must become the primary forum for job-embedded professional learning, not just a place for completing tasks. Learning from colleagues about teaching practices—not based on personal preference but because evidence clearly demonstrates their impact on student learning—gives teams the greatest opportunity to change, enhance, and build teachers' instructional competence.

A lack of time can cause teams to rush over this action in the cycle of learning process and therefore not reap the full benefits. Teams can become highly task-completion oriented, sacrificing the opportunity to have in-depth discussions about the most impactful teaching practices as they rush on to the next phase of the cycle of learning. For example, we have worked with a team in which it was evident that some teachers were exceptional in helping students learn to read and comprehend what they were reading. Within the same team, other teachers were uncertain about what they needed to do. If the team's meetings didn't allow time for teachers having the greatest impact on the reading skills of their students to share their teaching practices, the other less-impactful teachers would have been denied the opportunity of learning from their colleagues and enhancing their teaching practice. This would ultimately mean condemning the students in their classes to learn at a lower level.

The aim of this cycle of learning process is to make the most impactful teaching practices the common teaching practices across all team members by providing teachers with opportunities to learn from one another. As Marzano (2017) reminds us, teaching is both a science and an art. This action allows teachers to capitalize on both these aspects. Successful teachers use a wide range of teaching practices to improve student learning. This action and its associated tasks encourage teachers to work collaboratively to identify which practices are the most impactful and then investigate how they might incorporate them into their own teaching repertoire to enhance their students' learning. Done properly, this process allows teachers to feel valued and respected for what they do in their classrooms and to continually learn with and from their colleagues as they explore teaching practices and approaches to ensure high levels of learning for their students.

Teachers Make Excuses for Lack of Student Learning

Another challenge that can be encountered at this phase of the process is the temptation for teachers to advance external excuses for the learning results of students in their cohort or class rather than use the learning data to reflect deeply on the impact of their teaching practice.

We are realists and understand that some student cohorts can be more difficult to teach than others. These difficulties can be the result of a wide range of issues. High-performing collaborative teams also recognize and acknowledge this but never allow it to become an excuse for not examining their individual and collective teaching practices and attempt to overcome these issues. When a high-performing collaborative team has a difficult cohort to teach, members draw even more heavily on their team's collective expertise and work harder to identify teaching practices that have the greatest impact on improving the learning of their students.

A lack of time can exacerbate this, but collaborative teams that are time poor don't have time to blame and agonize about factors over which they have no control. High-performing collaborative teams recognize and honor the time that they *do* have and use the time available at collaborative team meetings to discuss what they *do* have control over: their teaching practice. They prioritize the right work to make the most of the time that they have.

Learning Data Aren't Used to Monitor Progress Toward the Team SMART Goal

Collaborative teams need to be mindful that at this point of the cycle of learning they should use the learning data, gathered from common quick checks, to monitor the progress they are making toward the achievement of their SMART goal.

If they don't frequently check on their progress throughout the process, teams have to wait until they administer the postassessment to see whether they have achieved their SMART goal. At that point, it is too late to go back and change things. Teams need to be able to identify quickly when things aren't working and intervene to change their teaching practices as soon as they have that information. Making these ongoing adjustments increases the likelihood that teams will achieve their SMART goal at the end of the cycle of learning.

Action 9
Adopt the Most Impactful Instructional Practices

Changing teaching practice in ways that benefit students means constant checking that such changes are having the desired impact. Effectiveness is context-dependent, so the knowledge and skills to check the impact must become part of the cycle of inquiry.

—Helen Timperley, 2009, p. 24

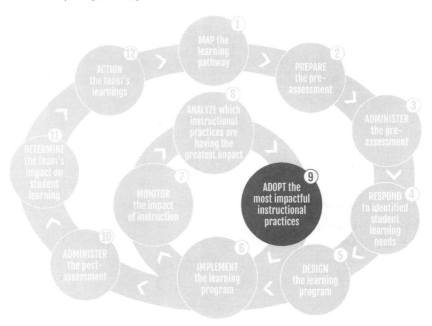

It's one thing to identify practices that truly make a difference and another to then do something with that knowledge. No cycle of learning can be considered action research unless action is taken. This action includes all team members adopting the approaches proven to be the most successful in classrooms and implementing rigorous systems of intervention to target learning at the point of need. By monitoring their progress and reviewing their learning goals, students also learn about what works best for them through the learning and teaching process. Celebration continues to play a key part in motivating student learning in this action.

The Tasks

Implement the Most Impactful Strategies in All Team Members' Classrooms

Having identified, explored, and learned about the teaching approaches that have proven to have the greatest impact on student learning, it is incumbent on all team members to ensure that they incorporate these approaches into their teaching practice. This ensures that all students benefit from the proven approaches.

The individual and collective impact these adjustments have on student learning should be monitored constantly and further changes must be made if they do not have the desired effect. Measuring the ongoing effects of changes to their practice allows team members to continue to learn more about and adjust their teaching until they achieve the maximum impact.

As a Team, Implement Interventions to Enhance Student Learning

This action also compels teams to take a more targeted approach to intervention by providing greater time and support to those students who need it. It assumes that a system of intervention has been put in place at the whole-school level to provide teams with the time needed to implement what Austin Buffum, Mike Mattos, and Chris Weber (2011) call *Tier 2 interventions*.

Tier 2 interventions require the teaching program related to the current cycle of learning to be paused. While teachers continue to implement new skills, knowledge, and dispositions from other areas of the curriculum, additional time and support must be provided within the timetable to both support students to reach the standard and provide extension and enrichment to those who already have. In the truest sense of the word, teachers intervene by coming to the students at their points of understanding and providing what's needed to bridge the gap.

Common assessment data provide a clear indication of which students need extra time and support and which students need enrichment and extension. Targeted intervention sessions built into the master timetable can then be used to ensure this happens.

All students receive Tier 2 interventions at their specific point of need. This avoids some students moving on to new learning while others miss out because they are involved in "remedial" sessions. This is unfortunately a hallmark of more traditional ways of catering to students who are not learning at the expected level.

The extra time and support students receive relates specifically to the prioritized standards and related learning goals. Realistically, teams can't intervene in this manner in all areas of the curriculum. They must instead target their interventions to the learning goals detailed on the learning pathway, those the school and team have deemed as essential for students to reach proficiency in by the end of the cycle of learning. The times we have seen Tier 2 interventions work best are when the school leaders mobilize all available resources and personnel to support students during Tier 2 sessions. With this additional support, collaborative teams are able to target the learning needs of students more specifically.

Intervention should never be seen as an approach only for those students who are falling behind. Rather, intervention provides the opportunity for additional time and support to be given to all students, regardless of where they are in their progress. Learn more about the concept and different tiers of intervention in *Collaborative Systems of Support: Learning for All* (Weber, Hierck, & Larson, 2016).

Use Quick Checks to Identify the Effectiveness of Interventions and Adjust Teaching Practice Accordingly

It is important that teams continue to use quick checks to monitor whether the Tier 2 intervention practices they employ are having the desired impact on student learning. This task ensures teachers maintain their focus on monitoring, adjusting, and refining their teaching practice in line with the information they collect. Enhancing both student and teacher learning remains at the heart of this action.

Identified by these quick checks, students who exhibit a lack of proficiency in the intended skills, knowledge, and dispositions despite the provision of extra time and support through Tier 2 interventions may need a different teaching approach than initially tried by their own teachers. Job-embedded professional learning is a pivotal component of this phase of the cycle of learning process. With this in mind, collaborative teams need to investigate alternative teaching approaches that might serve these vulnerable students more effectively and apply them, monitoring their effectiveness.

Have Students Continue to Monitor and Record Their Learning Progress, and Review and Revise Their Personal Learning Goals

Student voice and agency are essential aspects of the work. Involving students by asking them to reflect on the progress they have made and identify what has assisted them and what has not is important. Collaborative teams should continue to investigate the many different ways students can review, record, and monitor their own learning—for example, through the use of student portfolios, logbooks, journals, rubrics, and learning charts.

Students need to actively monitor, record, discuss, and adjust their learning goals so that they can identify and understand the next steps on their continued learning journey. Students also need the opportunity to discuss the impact their thinking has on their learning as well as the impact of their teacher's approach to helping them. This continued student feedback is designed to inform teachers about what they might need to do to assist their students in their further learning (Grift & Major, 2020).

Celebrate Student Learning Growth

First highlighted in Action 7 (page 57), team members' continued commitment to celebrating the growth of student learning is important to a student's identity, his or her capacity for self-reflection, and the ongoing development of his or her self-esteem. It also places the emphasis of the student's experiences at school on learning.

Students benefit from celebrations of their continuing learning success. Celebrations during this phase of the learning cycle convey messages such as the following.

- You can learn and be successful here.
- No matter how hard things get, you have the support here to succeed.
- Learning itself is a rewarding and intrinsically satisfying process.
- Self-growth is more important than how you compare to someone else.
- Your learning can benefit you in many ways.
- You and your learning matter.

Implementation Challenges

Schools Don't Recognize a Need for a Systematic Response to Intervention

When school leaders abdicate their responsibility for creating systemwide structures to support intervention across their school, the impact that the cycle of learning process has on student learning is compromised. The fundamental purpose of any high-performing PLC is to ensure all students learn to high levels. This requires all stakeholders to take collective responsibility to do what they can to make this a reality. When this collective responsibility is embraced by all, there are no barriers to the creation of school structures that truly provide additional time and support for students.

Far too many times, we have witnessed collaborative teams doing all they can to ensure they provide extra time and support for students to gain the level of proficiency required, only to fall short because of a lack of structural support for intervention across their school. It is imperative that school leaders relentlessly search for ways to structure their school's timetable to provide additional time and support to intervene when it becomes apparent that, despite the collective efforts of teachers, some students are not learning to the required level of proficiency.

Unchangeable school structures are often the excuse for not providing this additional time and support, but in reality, it is those who create the structures and are unwilling to upset the status quo who stand in the way. The result is that these archaic, misaligned, and fixed structures remain despite being the very barriers to achieving high levels of learning for all students.

Students who are not mastering the at-standard content deserve a systematic approach that meets their learning needs. This cannot be achieved by collaborative teams alone. Rather, it requires a coordinated and systematic approach across the school with the allocation of additional resources to support the work of collaborative teams.

When we see collaborative teams struggling to achieve high levels of learning for all students, we know that the necessary structures and intervention practices probably aren't in place at the whole-school level to support their endeavors and hard work. This is monumentally problematic because the greatest gains in student achievement occur in schools where there is a systematic, whole-school response to intervention (RTI) embedded into the school's structures.

Intervening when students do not learn is a moral obligation for any school committed to achieving high levels of learning for all students.

Intervention Is Delegated to Collaborative Teams

As we've already established, a lack of resources and intervention structures that allow collaborative teams to provide additional time and support to students who need it can slow progress. Collaborative teams can be fooled into believing they have Tier 2 interventions in place when really these sessions are no different from what they could provide in their own classrooms. The absence of additional personnel to enable teams to intensify the instruction for students who require additional support undermines their efforts. School leaders need to ensure human resources are maximized during Tier 2 intervention sessions to intensify the instruction.

Schools also need to ensure that Tier 2 intervention sessions are provided for in the master timetable. These blocks of time must be reserved for no new instruction to provide the opportunity for collaborative teams to target the specific learning needs of students in their cohort or subject with additional teaching assistance.

Student Grouping Lacks Flexibility

Teams struggle to remain focused on providing targeted support when quick checks aren't implemented or the information obtained from them is not fully used. Locking students into a group over a period of time or until a particular body of content has been taught does not constitute the collaborative work outlined in this and earlier actions. When students are locked into a group, the unspoken expectation is that they are not capable of learning the at-standard content and, therefore, aren't expected to. Streaming or tracking students in this way maintains the status quo. There is nothing to indicate that this practice leads to higher levels of student achievement. In fact, the evidence suggests that this practice has a detrimental effect on student learning (Hattie, 2012). In our experience, though it might work for the top group, it typically makes no real difference to the middle group and leaves the lower group considerably worse off.

The fine line between streaming and flexibly grouping students is one that we see crossed by schools time after time. The key to ensuring that groups remain flexible and truly serve student learning is responding to individual learning needs by using the information from quick checks. With this information, teams can make informed decisions about whether a student stays in a group or moves to another. The aim of any student grouping is to resolve the issue and get the student out of the group as soon as possible.

Some students may only need to be in a group for one session, while others will need several sessions before they can move on. The only way teachers can know this is by carrying out quick checks and constantly analyzing and monitoring those data. This assists collaborative teams to target the additional time, support, and resources to the relevant needs of their students and determines students' movement in and out of groups. The provision of additional time and support is a difficult structural issue for schools to address, but it is vital if they are to meet the individual and collective learning needs of all students.

When collaborative teams carry out this action and its associated tasks with fidelity and determination, there are high gains in student achievement. Committing to short-term, homogeneous, flexible groupings to target specific skill development is a productive and successful way to support the continued enhancement of student achievement.

Intervention Occurs Too Late

Some collaborative teams see intervention as something that happens at the end of a cycle of learning, rather than something that occurs continuously during the process. As illustrated in the diagrams of this stage in a cycle of learning, Actions 6 through 9 are repeated as new skills, knowledge, and dispositions are introduced and taught. This means that teams have ongoing opportunities to intervene and ensure students achieve high levels of learning throughout the process, not just at the end.

Teams can often believe that they have been successful by virtue of simply providing intervention. It is critical that collaborative teams monitor the impact and effectiveness of any intervention they provide to ensure they are closing gaps in student learning. Simply providing intervention isn't enough; interventions need to be monitored closely to ensure that they have the desired impact on student learning so that any necessary adjustments can be made to teaching approaches and intensity of instruction.

SECTION 3
Reviewing the Learning

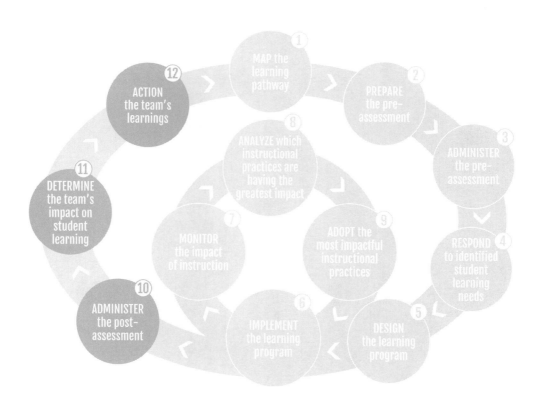

Action 10
Administer the Postassessment

Summative assessments can help teachers determine whether students are making adequate academic progress or meeting expected learning standards, and results may be used to inform modifications to instructional techniques, lesson designs, or teaching materials the next time a course, unit, or lesson is taught.

—Great Schools Partnership, 2013

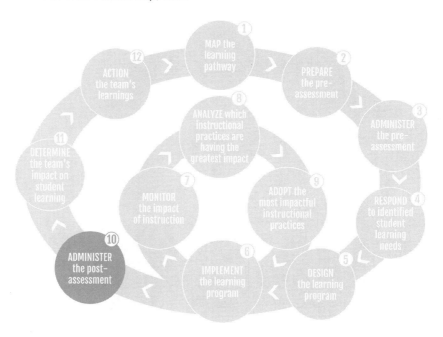

At this stage of the cycle of learning process, having used common quick checks to closely monitor the learning progress their students have been making, collaborative teams should have a good idea of the levels of learning they can expect their students to exhibit upon administering the postassessment. These quick checks will have also provided valuable information on the collaborative team's progress toward achieving the SMART goal set at the beginning of the cycle of learning. This action allows teams to continue to address the second critical question of the PLC at Work process: How will we know our students are learning? (DuFour et al., 2016).

The Task

Administer the Summative Assessment When Quick Checks Show the Smart Goal Is Close to Being Achieved

When teams determine through common quick checks that they are close to achieving their SMART goal and have taught all of the skills, knowledge, and dispositions related to the cycle of learning, it is time to administer the common postassessment developed in Action 5 (page 43).

Of course, the time that teams have available to devote to a cycle of learning is limited. However, it is important where possible that a team makes the decision about when to administer a postassessment based on the learning of its students, not simply because the time allocated for the cycle in question is close to expiring.

As is the case when administering the preassessment, it is important that teams have reviewed and committed to implementing this assessment in a common way. This will ensure that the learning data they collect are fair, valid, and reliable, and that their subsequent discussions and the conclusions they draw from the data accurately reflect student achievement.

Action 11
Determine the Team's Impact on Student Learning

In short, there is nothing more important in determining the effectiveness of a team than each member's understanding of and commitment to the achievement of results-oriented goals to which the group holds itself mutually accountable.

—Richard DuFour, Rebecca DuFour, Robert Eaker, and Thomas Many, 2006. p. 136

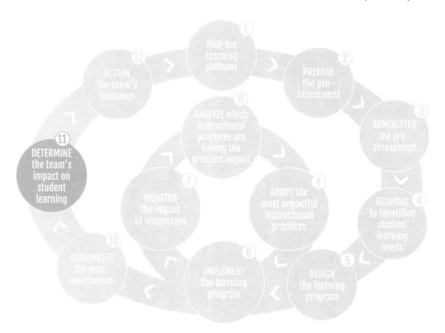

This action highlights the critical importance and role of the SMART goal in creating a basis for collaboration. Team members rely on one another to reach their shared SMART goal and then commit to further actions based on their level of success. This fosters a sense of collective responsibility for student learning while also enabling teams to formally monitor their impact and make informed decisions.

The Tasks

Analyze the Data to Check on the Team's SMART Goal

Determining a collaborative team's impact on student learning requires the team to analyze the data and measure students' learning growth. This will enable the team to make some decisions about what it needs to do next. If a team is close to or has achieved its SMART goal, then it will conclude the process and move on to the next cycle of learning. Conversely, if it finds that it is a long way short of its SMART goal, which should not be a surprise provided team members have been monitoring student learning with common quick checks, a team might decide to postpone the cycle of learning while it investigates ways to ensure that students reach the required level of proficiency.

Decide Whether to Continue, Conclude, or Postpone (and Later Revisit) the Cycle

If student learning data obtained through the postassessment show that a team is well short of achieving its SMART goal, it is an indication that team members' individual and collective teaching practices haven't been effective or strong enough to support students to make the progress required. When this occurs, the team will need to return to this cycle of learning later, having taken the time to upskill to ensure it is able to better support all students to learn the required skills, knowledge, and dispositions. Due to time constraints, this revisiting approach can only occur in areas deemed as the most critical and crucial for students' future learning success. The aim, of course, is to minimize the chance of this occurring by implementing strong teaching practices from the beginning of each cycle of learning.

There are many different options to consider when it is revealed there's a need for teachers to engage in further professional learning. These may include professional readings, attending professional learning sessions or courses, or observing colleagues who are getting better results and have obvious strengths in their teaching practice. It could also involve speaking with experts from within and outside the school community, inquiring into new approaches, and finding different ways to solve the instructional problems that teachers face.

When a team is close to achieving its SMART goal, it may decide to adjust its pacing guide and continue to implement the cycle of learning for a set number of sessions to achieve this goal. The pacing guide must remain flexible and should be adjusted depending on how a team is tracking. A more traditional curriculum planner would dictate that after the set time has expired, the team automatically moves on, regardless of the level of proficiency reached by students, but this does not support the work of collaborative teams on a mission to achieve high levels of learning for all.

All of the elements related to this task contribute to a team's ability to make a timely decision on whether it continues, concludes, or postpones the cycle of learning at this point in the process.

Celebrate Informally Individual and Collective Growth in Effective Teaching Practices

It should be remembered that through the whole cycle of learning process, students are encouraged to celebrate their own learning as well as the learning of their peers, both with their teachers and with one another. However, at this point, as they analyze the data they have collected, teachers have the opportunity to recognize the difference they have made with their fellow team members. During this phase of the cycle of learning process, it is important that team members take the time to recognize and celebrate their achievements in improving student learning and strengthening their own teaching practice.

Implementation Challenges
Time Becomes a Barrier to Decisions Made About Learning

A collaborative team's inability to adjust the time allocated for a cycle of learning can be a genuine barrier to completing this action. SMART goals are the trigger for determining whether a team is going to move on to the next cycle of learning or extend the current one to ensure that it achieves its goal. If a team is inflexible in making decisions about when a cycle of learning ends, student achievement can be compromised.

The reality of the tightness of some schools' curriculum planning often means teams cannot extend the time allocated for a cycle of learning. When this occurs, teams need to take a longer view and determine when there might be an opportunity for them to return to the cycle later in the year. In these instances, we suggest that collaborative teams pause the cycle of learning and find the time to return later so that students' learning in subsequent years is not negatively affected.

When schools have identified the most essential components of the curriculum by developing a guaranteed and viable curriculum, it is disingenuous for teams to move on with the learning program without giving students every opportunity to learn these essential components. Teams need to ensure that they understand there must be flexibility to allow opportunities for the cycle of learning to be extended. This will often require courageous but necessary discussions to be held. This flexible approach is absolutely crucial to prioritize a focus on learning over a focus on teaching.

Action 12
Action the Team's Learnings

At a Meeting

After you have determined and understood the growth of your students, you are in a position to assess the impact of your teaching and consider how well you have enabled your students to progress. This can give you the chance to learn what is contributing to learning and what might need to change and improve.

—State Government of Victoria, 2020

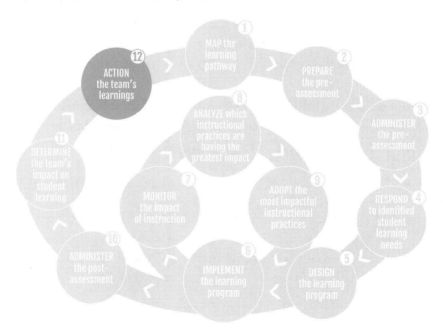

Once a team has collated the results of the postassessment, its members are then able to reflect more fully on what they have learned through the cycle of learning and carry this forward into the next cycle of learning.

As we have emphasized, we view the whole cycle of learning process as collaborative action research. The process means teachers are able to deliver content in a way that allows them, as collaborative team members, to investigate the strengths of their individual and collective teaching practice. As such, actioning the team's learnings is the crucial next step after teachers have reflected on the most successful teaching practices used in a cycle of learning, what they have learned by implementing them in their own classroom, and how they will ensure that they are embedded into their teaching practice.

The Tasks

Discuss What the Team Has Learned Through the Cycle of Learning and Identify the Most Effective Teaching Practices

In this phase of the cycle of learning, team members must again reflect on and celebrate the impact of their teaching practice on student learning. Team members also discuss the major things they have learned about their teaching practices, noting which practices should become part of their team's teaching pedagogy from this point onward.

Many of the teaching practices identified as being highly impactful may also be relevant to other subject areas and grade levels. As such, this phase of the cycle of learning process also provides the opportunity for teams to share specific, highly impactful teaching practices, validated by learning data, with other collaborative teams in their school. This allows team members' colleagues to benefit from the action research they have carried out as a team.

Celebrate Formally the Difference, Measured by Student Learning Growth, the Team Has Made Both to Individuals and to Groups of Students Through the Cycle of Learning

Team members should also take the time at this point to acknowledge the impact their efforts have had on student learning more formally. Actioning their teams' learning provides the more formal opportunity for individual teachers to be recognized for the improvements they have made to the learning of students in their classes. In doing so, teams identify the specific teaching strategies and approaches that have improved student learning and discuss future and further applications of these identified practices.

In high-performing PLCs, the schoolwide sharing and celebration of growth has become an important part of their ongoing job-embedded professional learning processes. It creates a culture of continuous learning where all educators at the school understand that it is everyone's duty to continually enhance his or her teaching competency to ensure high levels of learning for all students. This can happen in a multitude of ways, including staff meetings, professional learning forums, cross-collaboration opportunities, and other internal communication mechanisms.

Review and, Where Necessary, Adjust the Essential Learnings Associated With the Prioritized Standards

This phase of the cycle of learning process also provides the opportunity for teams to review and, where necessary, adjust the essential learnings associated with the prioritized standards that were the focus of the learning program. Through implementing a cycle of learning, collaborative teams may discover that some of the essential learnings were given a higher priority than necessary in the pacing guide or needed a higher priority than they were given. Teams may have even determined that there were skills, knowledge, or dispositions that needed to be taught that weren't included. These learnings should be documented and the learning program amended to reflect this so that teams that teach the cycle of learning in subsequent years benefit from what has been learned.

Each cycle of learning provides the opportunity for collaborative teams to contribute to and continually refine their school's guaranteed and viable curriculum, the development of which is an ongoing process. Making adjustments and modifications to the school's guaranteed and viable curriculum is an essential part of each cycle of learning if successive teams are to build on others' achievements.

Review and, Where Necessary, Adjust the Assessment Tools Associated With the Cycle of Learning

This is also an opportunity for teams to reflect on the assessment strategies and tools used in the cycle of learning. By answering questions such as "Were the assessments suitable for what we were teaching?" and "Were the assessments fair, valid, and reliable?" teams can rectify any issues and enhance their approaches before the cycle of learning is implemented again. This review is part of the action research process that ensures that each time the cycle of learning is implemented, it is implemented at a higher level than in any previous iteration.

Document and Carry Forward What Has Been Learned About Successful Teaching Practices to Subsequent Cycles of Learning

The final phase of the cycle of learning process draws together the various elements of the action research that teams have been conducting throughout and ensures that what they have learned is captured so that it strengthens the team's and school's practices. For example, over the course of the cycle of learning, team members may become more effective at using explicit instruction as a pedagogical approach, using think-alouds more strategically, or better supporting the independent work of their students with student conferences. The improvements in teaching practices that have been validated by the collected learning data can be discussed and clarified in this phase. Teams can then explore ways to incorporate these highly impactful approaches into upcoming cycles of learning and share their learnings with other colleagues so that their students can also benefit. Continuing to work in this way, collaborative teams become more skillful in implementing the process and persistently enhance their efficacy as a team. They learn by doing in the purest sense of the phrase.

Through the action research that is embedded in the cycle of learning process, teachers continuously improve their practice in their quest to achieve increasingly high levels of learning for all students. By making teachers' practices known and building collective responsibility for the learning of all students, school culture evolves into one that has a genuine focus on learning and recognizes that student learning can only improve if educators continue to evolve and strengthen their teaching practice—a culture that champions learning for all.

Implementation Challenges

Teams Fail to Carry Forward What They Have Learned to the Next Cycle of Learning

Teams struggle when they do not recognize that each cycle of learning builds on the previous one and that the process is part of greater continuous cycles of improvement. Even though collaborative teams learn a lot about their individual and collective teaching practice and the process of implementing a cycle of learning, they can often revert to their previous way of teaching or a previous implementation method in the next cycle.

These teams view each cycle of learning as discrete and separate events and don't transfer what they have learned—or perhaps don't even see how they could transfer what they have learned—into the next cycle of learning. Failing to capitalize on what they have learned means they lose the opportunity for continuous growth as individual teachers and as a team.

Teams Don't Take Enough Time to Reflect, or They Focus on the Wrong Things

In our work with schools and collaborative teams, we frequently see this phase of the cycle of learning process given only cursory or token consideration. In their haste to move on, get tasks done, or attend to other items of business, team members often do not allow themselves to take the time that deep, reflective practice requires.

It is important that teams' reflections center on their approaches to improving student learning and the teaching strategies that were adopted to enhance their practice. Teams must reflect on and draw meaning from the changes they made to their individual and collective practices to increase their impact on student learning. Further, they need to avoid reflecting solely on the activities that worked or didn't work, but rather focus on changes to the way they actually taught their students.

The Guaranteed and Viable Curriculum Stagnates

Some staff believe that, once developed, their guaranteed and viable curriculum is fixed and the best it can possibly be. However, this attitude means that staff misses opportunities to build on this foundation with genuine, ongoing review and revision of their curriculum by the people who deliver it.

Part of the adult learning and action research built into each cycle of learning is the opportunity for teams to assess their school's guaranteed and viable curriculum. During this phase, teams need to know they have the license to make suggestions and recommendations to school leaders about possible enhancements or changes that will ensure their school's guaranteed and viable curriculum remains as relevant, focused, and targeted as possible.

When teams know that this is an important part of their work and that they have permission to suggest enhancements based on their research, curriculum review isn't an event but instead becomes part of their school's ongoing process of continuous curriculum improvement.

Celebration Gets Forgotten

In some schools, the challenge is not to see celebration as a chore and something else that needs to be crossed off a to-do list. At times, celebration of what has been learned through a cycle of learning can also be overlooked because of perceived time constraints or because other tasks are deemed to be more important. However, celebrating teachers' individual and collective success in improving student learning allows teams to deeply reflect on what they have actually learned through the cycle of learning. Celebration ensures that these impactful teaching practices are more likely to become a part of a team's ongoing repertoire.

Our work with schools continues to highlight for us that educators do not learn solely from experience itself and that learning occurs at a much deeper level when teachers are able to process and reflect on their experiences with their colleagues. Celebrations compel teams to process what they have learned in a more formal and collaborative way.

Continuous school improvement is exhausting. Celebrations are an important way of motivating educators and maintaining their enthusiasm for the work required to progress their school's never-ending journey toward becoming a high-performing PLC. The responsibility for celebrations should be jointly shared between teams and school leaders.

Team Members Lack Understanding and Commitment to the Process

Time-poor teams often feel that the cycle of learning process is just a list of actions and tasks to get through, which can lead to their actions being driven by compliance rather than genuine commitment and the belief that the process is the best way to achieve high levels of learning for both students and teachers. At this phase of the process, this approach results in teams carrying out only a very superficial level of analysis of what they have learned through a cycle of learning, in turn meaning that they are unlikely to improve on their efforts in subsequent cycles.

These issues can be overcome if teams are supported to work through the process that truly assists them in overcoming the complex challenges associated with their everyday work. Working through the cycle with fidelity ensures teachers are focused on the work they value most: improving student learning. When teachers then experience success in their collaborative endeavors, their commitment to the process will increase.

Teams commit to the process more steadfastly when they see the impact it has on both student and teacher learning. This can only happen when they take the time to learn from what they have executed. Each cycle of learning provides the opportunity for teachers to incorporate what they have learned into their ongoing professional practice. To what extent they do so will depend on how they view the tasks. When these actions and associated tasks enable genuine and relevant professional learning to occur with their colleagues, teachers' individual and collective commitment to the process are strengthened.

SECTION 4
Adopting an Alternative Approach

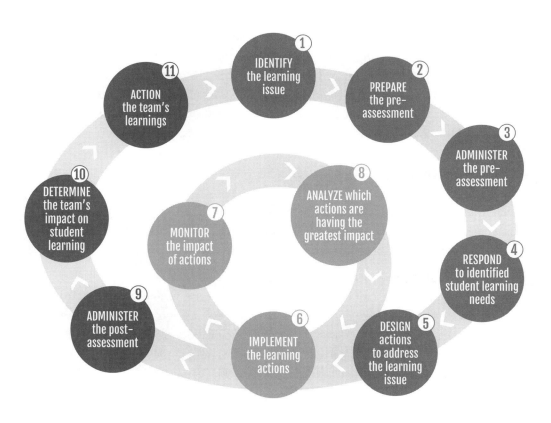

1. **IDENTIFY** the learning issue
2. **PREPARE** the pre-assessment
3. **ADMINISTER** the pre-assessment
4. **RESPOND** to identified student learning needs
5. **DESIGN** actions to address the learning issue
6. **IMPLEMENT** the learning actions
7. **MONITOR** the impact of actions
8. **ANALYZE** which actions are having the greatest impact
9. **ADMINISTER** the post-assessment
10. **DETERMINE** the team's impact on student learning
11. **ACTION** the team's learnings

Starting the Cycle of Learning With a Learning Issue

Our revised definition of a PLC, derived from that of DuFour and his colleagues (2016) and shared in the introduction to this book (page 1), is critical to the work of any high-performing collaborative team. The key element to this definition is that to be a genuine PLC, no matter how you structure them, collaborative teams must become the catalyst for higher levels of learning for both teachers and students.

The PLC at Work process asks schools to consider the following question when forming collaborative teams: Do team members have a shared responsibility for responding to issues around curriculum, assessment, and instruction in ways that enhance students' learning? This question checks the ability of each collaborative team to address the four critical PLC at Work questions, also noted in the introduction (page 1).

The cycle of learning process detailed in the first three sections of this book can only be truly implemented by collaborative teams that share responsibility for delivering common content. However, if a team is not aligned in this way, it is possible to carry out an alternative cycle of learning process centered on investigating a learning issue related to teaching practice. This alternative cycle of learning consists of eleven actions across three phases: (1) preparing, (2) implementing, and (3) reviewing the inquiry.

Though cycles of learning can be approached differently within schools that aren't able to establish teams on the basis of the common content they deliver, it is critical that it isn't seen simply as an easier or better option. This alternative approach, in which cycles of learning begin with a common learning issue rather than content, has simply been designed to support schools whose context prevents them from forming teams of teachers who deliver the same content. No school that takes on this alternative approach will improve student achievement to the same degree as a school that is fully committed to implementing the cycle of learning process outlined in the previous sections. When the organization of collaborative teams demands changes to school structures and culture, these teams will always be more impactful than those that cause minimal disruption. The PLC at Work process has been deliberately designed to alter the school status quo and shift the focus from content delivery to an unrelenting focus on learning.

In the PLC at Work process, collaboration is understood as a tool for whole-school transformation, not just a tool to change the work of teams (DuFour et al., 2016). The PLC at Work process is based on research that suggests schools attain higher levels of learning when they organize teams' collaborative endeavors around common content delivered during instructional periods, as these teams have closely aligned professional learning needs. As they are teaching similar content, team members can collectively respond to student learning needs by adjusting their instructional practices immediately. Their collaborative endeavors are informed by current evidence of student learning, which allows them to directly intervene to ensure high levels of learning for all.

Though this structure is the foundation of the PLC at Work process, we appreciate through our experience working with schools that many find it difficult to form teams in which members are responsible for teaching the same content. This makes the cycle of learning process outlined earlier in this book impossible to implement with fidelity and diminishes these collaborative teams' capacity to address the four critical PLC questions authentically.

Some of the reasons schools struggle to implement this preferred way of structuring teams include the following.

- Small schools don't have multiple teachers delivering the same content.
- If teachers are asked to form collaborative teams with colleagues from other smaller schools who teach the same content, it can be difficult for them to find genuine common goals because of the different contexts of their respective schools. These teachers often view these meetings as an extra burden on their already limited time.
- Teachers may deliver multiple content areas across a variety of grade levels and find it impossible to be in two or more collaborative teams at once. This is usually an issue at secondary schools.
- Online groups (often referred to as *electronic teams*) can be difficult, as they often involve greater complexity and require more organization issues to be overcome than meeting face-to-face.
- If teachers don't meet frequently enough (even when they share content), it becomes impossible to implement a cycle of learning process that starts with content. Teams need to meet for at least an hour each week to implement the process with fidelity.

Unable to form teams united by the content they deliver, many schools form what we refer to as *pseudo-collaborative* teams. Because these teams aren't formed with the focus and purpose of being a key agent for improving student learning through the enhancement of teaching practice, we do not consider them to be true collaborative teams.

If schools are unable to form teams that address the four critical PLC at Work questions because of their context, it is imperative that when organizing alternative team structures in their school, leaders ask the pivotal question, "Do team members have a shared responsibility for responding to the four critical questions in ways that enhance students' learning?" (DuFour et al., 2016). When this question sits alongside our revised definition of a PLC and guides the formation of collaborative teams in which members don't deliver common content, it ensures that the focus of these teams remains on the impact that members' individual and collective endeavors have on student learning through changes they make to their teaching practice.

To support schools that can't form teams that can respond to the four critical questions because they don't teach common content but still want to engage in the cycle of learning process to improve student outcomes by solving common learning issues, we propose the following five guiding questions. These questions ensure that collaborative teams whose members are not united by the teaching of common content are still able to focus their collective endeavors on enhancing teacher practice and student learning. The five guiding questions for teams formed on the basis of solving a common learning issue are as follows.

1. What student learning issue are we seeking to address?

2. How will we know we have addressed the student learning issue?

3. How might we overcome the issue?

4. What actions will we trial?

5. Which actions will we now adopt to enrich our instructional practices?

In this section, we outline the eleven key actions and associated tasks that these collaborative teams should carry out to address the five guiding questions. We also provide elementary and secondary school examples to illustrate what this process looks like in the field. These examples are drawn from our experiences of working with schools that have implemented the cycle of learning process starting from an identified learning issue.

Preparing the Inquiry

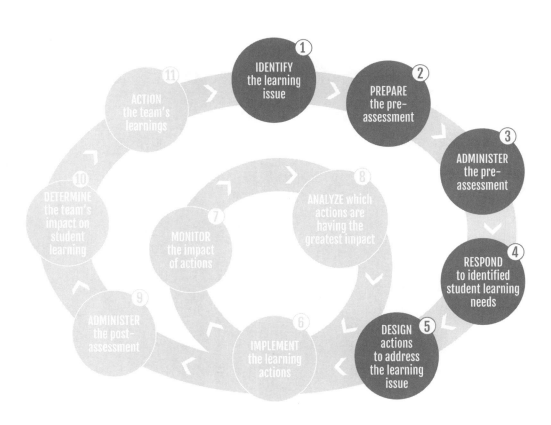

Action 1
Identify the Learning Issue

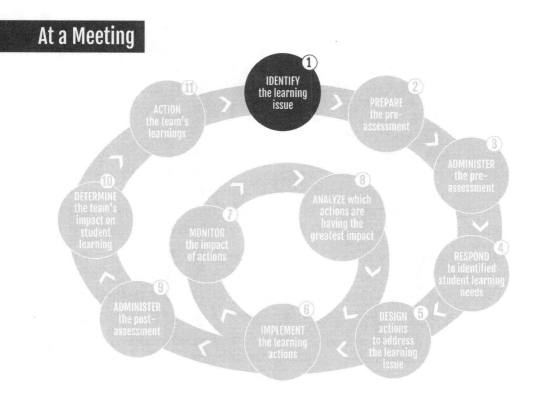

The Tasks

- Identify possible learning issues that team members want to address.
- Select a common issue and discuss why it is important and relevant to all team members.
- Identify learning data that indicate this is an issue for student learning.
- Identify any additional learning data that might need to be collected before a final decision can be made.
- Check this issue supports the achievement of school goals.
- Agree on a focus for the cycle of learning.

Identifying the learning issue that is to be the focus of a cycle of learning requires teams to share and explore possible learning issues that are relevant to each team member. The learning issue might be the basis for the formation of a team, or it may involve a collaborative brainstorming process that allows teachers to identify individual learning issues that are relevant to their practice and then determine commonality with their fellow team members.

Team members need to be invested in the issue that they identify so that it forms the basis for genuine collaborative inquiry and action research. By discussing and exploring which learning issues offer the greatest potential for improving student learning in their respective classes, team members engage in a process that allows them to identify an area of inquiry that genuinely interests and excites them, thus providing real purpose and relevance to exploring possible ways that the issue might be addressed.

Once the learning issue that unites a team has been identified, it is important that members reflect on relevant individual and collective learning data to confirm that this is a genuine issue for their team and school. By reviewing relevant learning data, the team will gain a better understanding of why the selected learning issue warrants its collaborative problem-solving endeavors, enhancing members' commitment to the cycle of learning. This part of the process also assists teams in identifying whether any additional learning data need to be collected before a final decision is made.

A check to gauge the relevance and validity of the issue selected as the focus for a cycle of learning is to confirm that it supports the achievement of school goals. As collaborative teams are the "engines" of school improvement, a strong alignment between each team's focus and its school's goals is imperative.

Once the data have been analyzed and discussed and the issue's relevance to school goals has been confirmed, teams can then make a final determination on whether the proposed learning issue is worthy of collaborative action research. We have found that this is a crucial step for team motivation and success. When identifying the learning issue is given the time and attention required, team members are far more committed in their determination to address and solve this issue because it is relevant and important to them.

In the Field

Elementary

A physical education teacher, music teacher, and library teacher formed a collaborative team in their elementary school. They initially struggled to know what they should focus on when they came together, and meetings were generally consumed by discussions of student misbehavior.

While these debriefs were useful, the team facilitator felt their time together could be better used. She decided to conduct a meeting at which team members listed the specific issues that they felt were impacting on student learning in their respective classes. Through this discussion, members noticed that they were all concerned by the amount of instructional time lost in classes they took after recess or lunch breaks as they dealt with issues that had arisen in the yard. Anecdotal reports shared in this meeting suggested that they could lose up to half their instructional time, validating that this could be a learning issue worthy of further consideration and their collective investigation.

While one team member felt it was a significant issue, the other two weren't sure, so the team decided to collect some data to bring back to a future meeting. For a nominated period, the teachers noted the time they actually commenced their teaching in sessions held after a break as compared to those classes that didn't follow a break. Having devised a simple spreadsheet together, team members were able to quickly record the number of minutes they lost in each session and then calculate the average time lost per session.

Noting that a key goal in their school's strategic plan focused on student engagement in learning, the team then checked with the principal, who agreed that the identified learning issue would support the achievement of that school goal.

At a subsequent meeting, the team tabled and discussed the results. The members who had been unsure of whether this was a significant issue that impacted on student learning in their classes were convinced when they reflected on the data they had collected.

Secondary

In a moderately sized secondary school, the leadership team committed to the collaborative team process as a way to improve student learning across the school. One of the resulting collaborative teams was the science team. This team was made up of science teachers from grades 7 through 10 and met four times a term. The team's first job was to identify possible common learning issues that were impacting the students they served across those grade levels in science.

The whole school had a focus on improving literacy because data previously collected showed that student achievement in this area was low. Many assessments conducted throughout the school required students to demonstrate their understanding through written responses, and it was clear that literacy levels were affecting students' success in many subject areas. The school leaders felt that the most effective way of addressing this issue was through a collaborative approach.

The science teachers understood the importance of literacy, particularly written skills, because they are key to a student's capacity to demonstrate his or her knowledge, skills, and understanding of key science concepts. In their team's discussions, members recognized that all science subjects had written components that were integral to their curriculum and that written responses were prominent in their assessment tasks.

The data that science teachers had gathered from their previous assessments confirmed the issue of low literacy levels was impacting their subject area as well, with many complaining about their students' ability to compose written responses. Writing skills, therefore, seemed the natural starting place for this collaborative team's inquiry.

Action 2
Prepare the Preassessment

At a Meeting

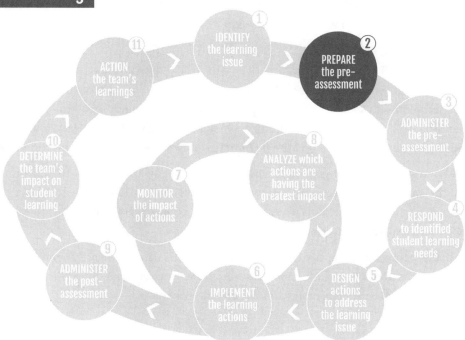

The Tasks

- Review any current data that relate to the issue being investigated. If no specific current data exist, develop a data-collection tool that will assess the current reality.

- Develop an end-of-cycle data-collection tool. (This may be the same as the initial data-collection tool.)

- Discuss the way that the data-collection tool will be implemented so that the data are valid and comparable.

- Identify how the data will be collated to be easily compared and analyzed.

It is important that teams focus on a genuine issue that results in measurable improvement in student learning. It is also imperative the data that teams collect measure the impact that the practices they adopt during this process have on this learning issue, so decisions can be made about what may need to be revised, refined, or completely changed in the future.

To achieve this, teams should first review any current data that relate to the issue being investigated. Using information that already exists and genuinely provides a clear and compelling rationale for why the identified learning issue could be a valuable focus saves time and allows team members to immediately move on to organizing the data in a way that will support the monitoring of their actions moving forward. If no specific current data exist, teams will need to develop a data-collection tool to collect the information they require to establish a baseline from which they will measure their impact.

Teams also need to consider how they will collect data at the end of the cycle of learning so that they can measure the impact they have had. This may be the same as the collection method used at the beginning of the cycle, but it might need to be different depending on the context of the inquiry. Once a method of data collection has been decided on, teams must develop both beginning- and end-of-cycle data-collection tools.

A team should then engage in discussion and dialogue around how to best implement the data-collection tool or tools, when this will be done, the level of support students will be given, and so on. This ensures the data collected are fair, valid, and reliable when compared across classes.

Finally, teams must identify how they will collate the data to be easily compared and analyzed. This needs to include consideration of the time required, who will assist, and how the data will be represented to allow for efficient analysis.

In the Field

Elementary

In identifying the learning issue that would be their focus, the team had already collected some data regarding the average amount of lesson time that was being lost to following up issues after breaks. The team members were confident that the data that they had collected were fair, valid, and reliable, and provided a baseline from which to measure the impact of any action they would then take in their respective programs.

They discussed the method that had been used to collect these initial data and decided that a similar process could be used at the end of the cycle of learning. The team then considered and ironed out a few issues with the way that the initial data had been collected and collated, noting points to consider when the process was implemented again. These agreed changes were recorded in the meeting minutes to ensure that they were remembered by all team members.

Secondary

The science team moved forward, having decided to focus on improving students' written responses in science so they could successfully demonstrate their understanding in class and through assessment tasks. This included helping students get better at short-answer tasks, short essays, and written responses to problems that teachers posed in class.

The collaborative team reasoned that state- or federally collected whole-school data were too general to use as a way of monitoring student progress and instead decided to generate a clear criterion for quality written responses in science. The team determined that this would be represented as a ten-point scale with which they could assess and track students' writing skills. By doing this, the team ensured that students across a wide range of competencies, regardless of grade level, were catered to. The ten-point scale that was developed also included benchmarks for students at the end of grades 7 through 10, making the tool relevant to every member of the team. They used the English department's grade 7 to 10 writing continuum to assist them in the development of their scale, saving time by capitalizing on the expertise of their colleagues.

Action 3
Administer the Preassessment

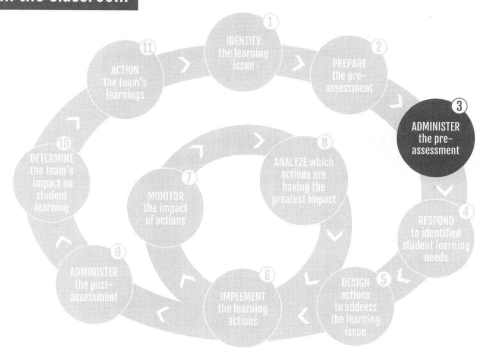

The Task

- Administer the preassessment (if data don't already exist).

Once a team has decided on the data it will collect, members should then administer the agreed-on data-collection tool to assess their students' current learning reality.

Teams are likely to be more successful and less overwhelmed when they plan in advance. Those that don't plan in advance to collect data (we suggest at least three weeks prior to carrying out Action 6, page 117) often end up collecting information at the same time as they attempt to implement the proposed actions. This may compromise the process, render the action research superficial because shortcuts will be made due to time pressures, and add unnecessary stress to team members' already busy schedules.

When teams don't gather data with enough lead time, members often come to view this part of the cycle of learning as an add-on rather than a valuable part of their role as teachers within a PLC. This can lead to a lack of commitment and belief in the collaborative team process.

In the Field

Elementary

Having already established baseline data for their individual classes, the team had been able to determine that specialist teachers lost an average of sixteen minutes of learning time in sessions conducted after students returned from a break. This could also be compared to similar classes taught in sessions not following a break, in which they lost an average of six minutes.

Secondary

Once the team members had committed to the identified learning issue, they decided to give students a fifteen-minute written task as their baseline data-collection tool. They each committed to bringing written work samples into the next meeting to begin plotting them against their previously developed ten-point scale.

The science teachers then implemented the fifteen-minute assessment task to gather their baseline data and assist in the formulation of their SMART goal. They decided to use the same assessment task at the end of the year with a different writing prompt to measure progress.

Action 4
Respond to Identified Student Learning Needs

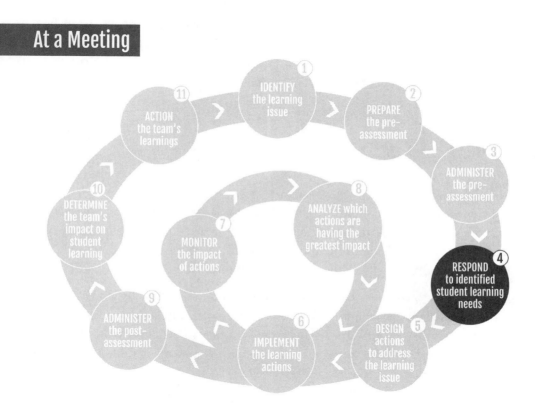

The Tasks

- Discuss the initial data to confirm the identified learning issue is a valid area of investigation.
- Develop a team SMART goal based on the level of improvement being aimed for by the end of the cycle of learning.
- Research possible actions to be taken to address the identified issue.

Once a team has collected data regarding the learning issue it intends to address, it will be ready to respond to identified student learning needs. This involves team members analyzing the data collected to identify specific areas in which change could help to resolve the learning issue. These data also provide the team with a baseline from which to measure its level of impact over the course of the cycle of learning. This discussion allows any further issues to be identified, and also helps teams to clarify the direction and focus of the upcoming cycle of learning.

Once a team has clarity and specificity regarding areas it wishes to address through the cycle of learning, the next task is to research possible actions it might take. This involves members exploring relevant research, which can include discussing with colleagues from within or outside their school community how they may have successfully addressed similar issues, investigating evidence-based practices outlined in articles or books, and reflecting on the findings of previous cycles of learning. Teams should be tenacious in exploring possible strategies, practices, and approaches that have potential for addressing their learning issues.

In the Field

Elementary

The team continued to discuss the initial data to clarify and determine what would be an achievable but challenging goal for reducing the average amount of teaching time lost after breaks. As a result of their discussions, the team members formalized their goal and came to an agreement about when they thought this goal could be achieved.

One teacher argued that the average time lost in classes following a break should be the same as in classes that don't, which caused rigorous discussion and countering points of view to be put forward. As this action was carried out close to the end of the first semester, the team members took into account the number of times that they, as specialist teachers, would take each class as well as the number of sessions that would be lost to whole-school activities when finalizing their timeline.

As a result of these discussions, the team was able to decide on the following SMART goal.

> By the end of the year, specialist teachers will have reduced the average amount of teaching time lost in classes following a break from sixteen minutes to eight minutes, as determined through the use of the data-collection tool developed previously by the team.

As the meeting concluded, the team members set themselves the task of doing some online research into ways to settle students into their learning quickly and engagement strategies that could be used in the initial stages of their lessons to reduce the amount of lost teaching time.

Secondary

At their next meeting, the team members brought all of their work samples and began to plot students along the ten-point scale. They decided to make the process as manageable as possible by only assessing the students who had been below proficiency in writing in the previous year, as demonstrated in their end-of-year reports. Their assessment confirmed that improving student written responses was definitely necessary. They found it reassuring to have their view supported by their own data.

Having analyzed student achievement levels from previous end-of-year reports to ensure that the goal would be attainable and results oriented, the team then established the following SMART goal.

> By the end of the year, we will have increased the proportion of students achieving four or more on the ten-point scale that represents their end-of-year mark in each science subject by 25 percent. This will mean 125 more students finishing the year at standard or above for their subject.

The team believed that a focus on helping students to develop deeper, richer, and ultimately more effective written responses would improve their capacity to complete high-stakes common assessment tasks that would contribute to their end-of-year mark at a higher level. For example, at the end of the year, a common assessment task worth 25 percent of a student's overall mark in biology would be predominantly made up of short responses to questions. With improvement in students' ability to express themselves through writing, the team predicted that there would be a direct improvement in their overall grades.

As the meeting concluded, the team members set themselves the task of doing further professional reading and online research into possible ways of improving their teaching of writing effective responses.

Action 5
Design Actions to Address the Learning Issue

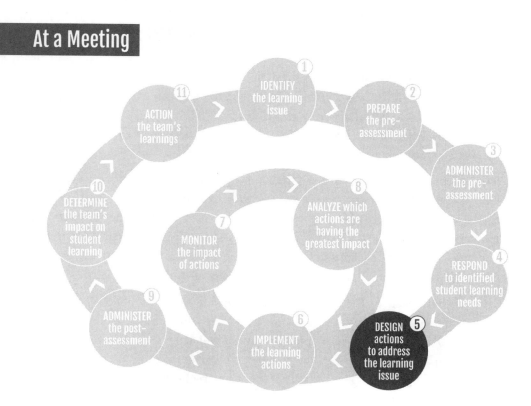

The Tasks

- Discuss the research-informed actions that have been identified that might improve the learning issue being focused on.

- Identify any other possible actions that team members feel might improve the issue being focused on.

- Agree on which of the possible actions will be implemented by the whole team or by individual team members.

- If applicable, discuss possible ways to communicate the proposed actions with students.

- Develop any resources necessary to implement the agreed actions.
- Decide on the quick checks that will be used to monitor the impact of the actions to be taken.

Designing actions to address a learning issue requires collaborative teams to commit to implementing specific approaches as a result of their preliminary discussions. This action and its associated tasks are what separates collaborative teams that are genuinely working through the process from teams looking for a quick fix or that simply rebadge their team without actually changing the work they do. Many so-called collaborative teams begin their work by immediately planning the actions they will take or roll out actions tried previously in a desperate attempt to maintain the status quo. The tasks outlined in Actions 1–4 prevent this from occurring and are necessary prerequisites for designing the actions to address a learning issue.

During this action, a collaborative team must discuss the practices previously researched and investigated that it believes will improve the identified learning issue. This requires team members to base decisions on research from the field of education, taking into account their particular context and any professional knowledge gained through previous cycles of learning they may have undertaken.

This is also an opportunity for team members to brainstorm and suggest any other possible practices they feel might improve the learning issue. This ensures all avenues have been exhausted before a team reaches consensus and commits to possible actions. Team members can also gain clarity here on which of the practices decided on will be implemented by the entire team and which might be implemented by individual members. This provides a genuine point for comparison between practices trialed.

Given the importance of students' understanding and ownership of their learning, it is important for team members to discuss how they will communicate their plans with their students. Whether this is applicable or not will depend on the actual learning issue. Where applicable, we strongly advocate team members to share with students the rationale, expectations, and possible approaches they might undertake as they implement the cycle of learning.

Once a team has clarity around the practices it will implement, it is important that it explores and identifies the human and nonhuman resources it will need for successful implementation. If team members feel they require resources they don't have access to or can't locate, they may need to develop their own.

Given that the inquiry process needs to be both manageable and viable, collaborative teams should also design quick checks to enable teachers to collect information on the impact of the actions they trial during the cycle of learning. These quick checks provide valuable information, allowing teams to monitor their impact as they implement a cycle of learning rather than having to wait until the end of the cycle.

Two quick checks we have seen used well in these contexts are *gray areas* and *60-second windows*, both of which we outline here.

Gray Areas

Ask students to outline what they didn't quite understand, referred to as the *gray area*, and have them propose what they think might help them to understand it better next time. As a collaborative team, review these gray areas so that you can clarify, correct, or elaborate as necessary before the next stage of learning.

60-Second Windows

During the last few minutes of a lesson, ask students to record the following on two separate sticky notes.

1. The most important thing they learned
2. The thing they understood the least

Students should spend just sixty seconds on these notes, minimizing this strategy's time impact on other teaching practices. As with the gray areas quick check, review this information at a collaborative team meeting before the next stage of learning and clarify, correct, or elaborate so any misunderstandings can be addressed.

In the Field

Elementary

At a subsequent meeting, team members reported back on the outcomes of their research. Each member briefly outlined some of the practices that they had learned about and summarized them on some large sheets of paper. One team member had spoken to some of the classroom teachers at the school and added the strategies he had gathered to the list. The teachers who lost the lowest amount of time on average also contributed the strategies they were already using in their classes to some success. As the discussion and presentation continued, the team developed and recorded a comprehensive list.

The team members then selected possible strategies they might implement in their own program from the comprehensive list. By the end of the meeting, each team member had identified three individual strategies he or she was going to trial during the cycle of learning and agreed on a common strategy that all members would implement.

They then worked together to further explore the common strategy. This strategy involved establishing a *car-parking* system to allow the teachers to list any student issues at the start of each session following a break. They then decided how this would look and be used in the classroom so that each specialist would use the strategy in the same way. To gain clarity and confidence in implementing the strategy, the teachers role-played the way that the new system would be introduced in their respective subject areas. With time left over in their meeting, they also developed posters outlining the strategy in student-friendly language for their classrooms and the gym, where the physical education teacher took her classes.

Team members committed to prepare the necessary resources for the other strategies they were going to implement in their programs outside the scheduled meeting time. An agreed timeline and a plan were established to guide their implementation of this cycle of learning.

The team discussed the way that teachers would involve the grades 3 through 6 students in their investigation. It was decided that they would devote the start of the first lesson in semester two to outlining the problem that they were trying to overcome and share their SMART goal with their students. Possible ways of doing this were put forward, and a common approach was agreed on.

As the meeting concluded, the team discussed ways to check on the impact of the strategies being used. It was decided that the process used for collecting the initial data was quick and efficient, and so team members agreed to implement this again at the end of weeks five, ten, and fourteen of the second semester. They also set a date for collecting the end-of-cycle learning data: four weeks before the end of the school year, given the hectic nature of end-of-year commitments.

Secondary

In the meeting, each team member gave a three-minute summary of his or her research into effective written responses. Commonalities about what the members found were noted and summarized at the end of their reporting back. They discovered that using reflection time at the end of their lesson more purposefully could really help their students. Their research indicated that having their students write down their key learnings from the lesson on a regular basis could be an effective way to develop both their writing skills and scientific understanding. All teachers indicated that they hadn't been using reflection time in their lessons in this way, and it particularly appealed to the teachers who believed a constructivist approach to learning was conducive to a deeper understanding of science.

Team members found other helpful ideas such as using frequent written exercises (outside of the textbook) that asked the students to capture their thinking. They also discussed the importance of balancing the use of written responses with providing time for students to engage in practical activities. Overall, however, everyone was convinced that by providing more time for students to write in class, these strategies would help them to achieve their goal.

The team members designed an implementation plan based on the ideas they had shared. They committed to incorporating more written response time during class, especially during the last ten minutes of a lesson, which they referred to as *reflection time*.

They discussed the need to ensure that what they asked students to do aligned to the type of writing that would be required when students were being assessed, particularly in the common assessment tasks that would contribute to the overall score students would receive. They agreed to trial these approaches in their individual classrooms and then come up with more specific ideas for using this ten-minute reflection time. They also discussed and committed to other ways of building writing exercises into their weekly program.

Part of their collaborative discussions centered on possible ways they could share their goal with their students. They felt it was important that students knew their teachers were supporting them to write in ways that would assist them when it came time to complete common assessment tasks. This would enable students to understand the purpose of new approaches their teachers might implement, while also being an opportunity for teachers to send the message that they genuinely care about their students' understanding and achievement in science.

The team researched additional ideas about teaching writing in subjects that were not traditionally literacy based. The teachers collected examples from different websites and also contacted the assessment and reporting coordinator to ask for sample assessments that included short-answer responses and short-essay exemplars. They also pooled their own teaching materials that related to written responses in science and discussed how they used them in their teaching practice.

The final commitment the team made was to use written responses completed during reflection time as quick checks through the course of the next term. This would allow team members to monitor the impact their efforts were having on the quality of identified students' written responses.

Implementing the Inquiry

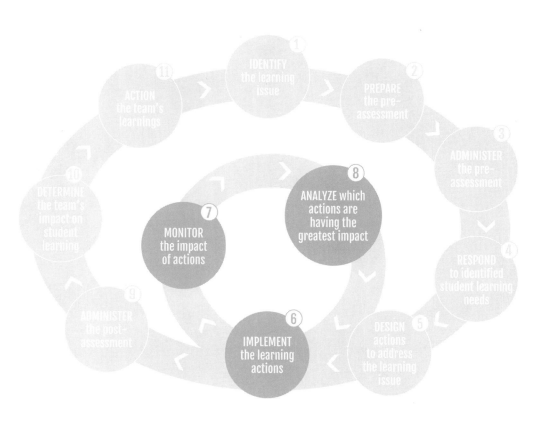

Action 6
Implement the Learning Actions

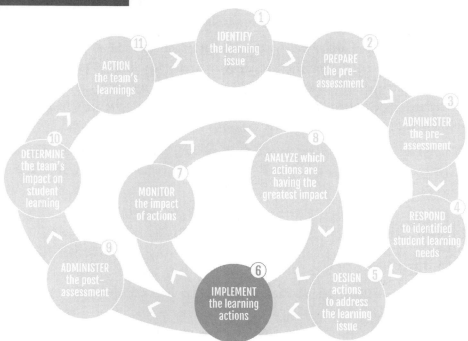

The Tasks

- Share the initial data with students.
- Have students set specific personal goals related to the issue being investigated, if applicable.
- Implement the agreed-on actions.

Once a team has determined and designed the actions that will be carried out in classrooms, team members are ready to implement those learning actions. This is when teams first implement the practices and strategies that they will monitor.

Building on Action 5 (page 109), we have found that sharing learning issues with students can alert them to possible changes to practices that they have been familiar with. Unannounced changes have the potential to create anxiety, concern, and confusion for students. This might be overcome by sharing the initial data or SMART goal with students. This sends the message to students that teachers are continuous learners too. Some learning issues might allow students to set related personal goals. Where this is possible, this allows students to become more directly involved in the cycle of learning and promotes the notion of student voice and agency.

Teams may instead prefer to treat the cycle of learning as a blind investigation and not inform students of the learning issue they are trying to address. This is usually governed by the nature of the learning issue that the team is inquiring into. This should be discussed and clarified before decisions are made about how team members will implement the cycle of learning in their classrooms.

This phase of the cycle of learning is itself cyclical, as a team incorporates different strategies, approaches, and practices into its members' regular teaching programs and monitors their impact.

In the Field

Elementary

During their first lessons in semester two, the teachers explained the learning issue that they were focusing on to their students, sharing the amount of learning time that was currently being lost and what they were hoping to reduce this to. They also provided a visual representation of this information with an agreed-on chart.

To complement their SMART goal, teachers decided to have the students in each grade level determine a target time reduction that they hoped to achieve by the midsemester break. This was to ensure each class was engaged and involved by having committed to their own goal. These class goals were displayed below the chart, which also showed the team's goal.

Specialist teachers then continued to deliver their normal programs, incorporating and monitoring the agreed strategies as they had discussed.

Secondary

Each science teacher shared with his or her students the overall data that led to the focus on improving written responses. They also shared the team SMART goal and introduced learning logs and an online learning management system.

In each class, teachers had their students set relevant learning goals related specifically to how they would improve the quality of their written responses. These incorporated elements such as sequencing ideas, spelling, correctly using grammar and punctuation, displaying clarity of ideas, summarizing thinking, and understanding writing prompts.

Each of the team members then went about incorporating his or her ideas, strategies, and approaches into the weekly lessons. Team members made a commitment to check on the impact of the approaches they were using by bringing work samples to their next scheduled meeting, which was six weeks away.

They specifically introduced written responses into the reflection time of each lesson. They also increased their use of written tasks in other aspects of their program, using the following strategies.

- Having pairs of students take turns writing down each other's reflections on an aspect of the content covered in the session
- Having students summarize in writing the most important information they were learning about, framing their thoughts through three critical points, two important points, and one nice-to-know point

Action 7
Monitor the Impact of Actions

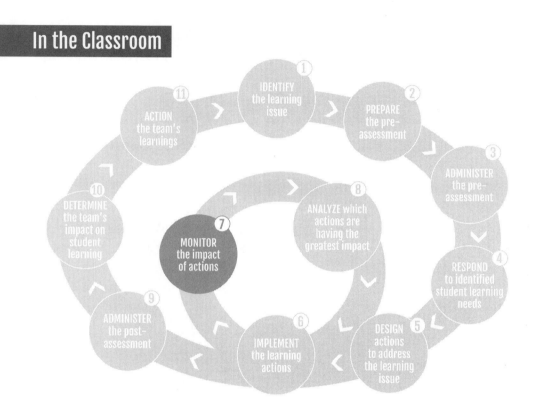

The Tasks

- Carry out frequent quick checks to continually monitor the impact of the actions being taken.

- Provide continual feedback to students on their progress in relation to the issue being addressed, if applicable.

- Ask students to monitor, record, review, and revise their personal goals, if applicable.

- Celebrate improvement as a result of the actions taken.

Monitoring the impact of actions requires educators to constantly evaluate the impact that changes in their practice have on the identified learning issue. Action research methodology is about impact, and the closer this impact is monitored, the more immediately teachers can adjust their practice based on the data they collect.

By carrying out frequent quick checks—using techniques such as those mentioned in Action 5 (page 109)—to continually monitor the impact of their actions, individual educators should collect tangible evidence to take back to collaborative team meetings for discussion.

If applicable, educators can also use this information to provide continual feedback to the students in their classrooms on their progress in relation to the issue being addressed. This immediate feedback shows students not only where they are on their own learning journey but also the impact of the implemented actions on their learning, helping them to see the value of learning as an ongoing process.

The evidence collected through these quick checks can also be used by students to monitor their own learning progress. Students who have set personal learning goals can use this evidence to continually review and revise their goals, a practice that supports students to develop a growth mindset.

This stage of the cycle of learning also provides teams with the opportunity to recognize and celebrate student learning progress as a result of the actions they have taken. Frequent and genuine celebration serves to continually remind students—and teachers—of the progress they are making and inspires them to continue in their endeavors. Celebration of student progress highlights that everyone can continuously improve when they put in the required effort.

In the Field

Elementary

At the start of each class, the specialist teachers reminded their students of the learning issue they were addressing and the goals that the team and students had set. As they had decided to record the time lost in each class on an ongoing basis, this update was also given to students at the start of each lesson. Where applicable, the specialist teachers had the class review and adjust their weekly goals based on their results from the previous week.

This review at the start of each lesson provided the opportunity to celebrate each class's progress toward achieving its goals. Teachers also started publicly acknowledging specific student behaviors that were contributing to their success, knowing this public celebration would further motivate other students. For example, "I noticed that when James entered the room today, he immediately sat on the floor and had his eyes to the front. Top effort, James. You're helping us reach our goal."

Secondary

As the science teachers approached reflection time in a more rigorous fashion, they also started to use the information they were able to collect to provide feedback to students at the beginning of the next lesson. The grades 7 and 9 teachers collected students' written responses at the end of each lesson to determine where more time might need to be spent in the following lesson with either the whole class or individual students to improve the quality of these responses.

This ongoing mechanism for checking in on their students' understanding made it possible for team members to share successes that their classes and students were having, while also providing impetus for more focused teaching in areas they were able to identify as being in need.

Action 8
Analyze Which Actions Are Having the Greatest Impact

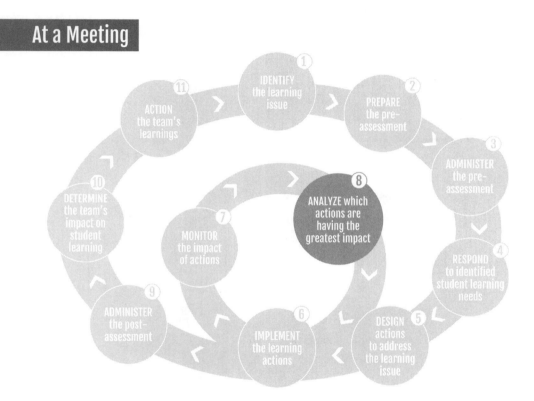

The Tasks

- Identify successful and not-so-successful actions as revealed by quick checks.
- Adjust the actions being implemented accordingly, implementing the most successful actions in all team members' classrooms.
- Check on the progress toward achieving the team SMART goal.

Analyzing which actions are having the greatest impact sits at the heart of action research. Using the information collected through quick checks, educators are able to determine the impact of the practices and strategies they have implemented. This is the stage of the cycle of learning in which the process truly becomes job-embedded professional learning because educators seek to better understand how their actions have affected the learning issue. When done well, this process of inquiry transforms both educators' instructional practice and student learning.

At this stage, collaborative teams must analyze the information they have collected through quick checks, using this data to identify what is working for their students and what is not. The evidence of impact, or lack thereof, then becomes the catalyst for discussion and continued action, with educators typically taking on others' successful practices or strategies. Subsequent discussions should then focus on how team members can support their colleagues in adopting these successful practices. For example, a teacher may invite another to observe how he or she delivers a successful practice in his or her classroom.

Another task associated with analyzing the actions having the greatest impact requires collaborative teams to check on their progress toward achieving their SMART goal. Monitoring this progress gives teams the information they need to make any necessary adjustments so that they reach their goal. These checks may also act as a catalyst for a team stretching itself even further if monitoring shows that it has attained its goal with time remaining in a cycle of learning.

In the Field

Elementary

The specialist teachers brought the data that they had collected during the first five weeks of the term to their midsemester meeting and analyzed the information to determine which strategies were proving to be the most impactful.

The team quickly reviewed the ways that members were using the car-parking system and determined that they all were implementing it in the agreed-on manner. This meant that differences in the data were due to the other individual strategies teachers were implementing.

In their analysis of the data, it was discovered that one teacher had achieved a greater reduction in lost time than the other two teachers. The team facilitator had this teacher explain the strategy he or she had been using to the other team members, who decided that they would trial this strategy in their classes to see if it produced a similar reduction in lost time. The teacher who had already implemented this strategy agreed to continue and also chose a new strategy from those that the team had tabled in Action 5 (page 109) to trial in his or her program.

The team members collated their data and determined the average time lost across all classes following a break. Checking this result against their SMART goal, they noted that although they had reduced the amount of lost teaching time, they hadn't yet achieved their goal.

The team committed to follow the adjusted plan over the remaining weeks of the semester.

Secondary

When the next meeting came around, the teachers brought along examples they'd collected of students' written responses and started to identify the impact that their focus on increasing the use of written responses was having. As they examined the samples, they noticed some improvements, particularly in some of the classrooms. Their analysis identified which strategies seemed to be working better than others, and they inquired further into why this might be happening.

Using the ten-point scale developed earlier, the team plotted students' positions based on the collected written samples. The dialogue centered on what the students had demonstrated and how they'd progressed—or hadn't—in relation to the criteria across all grade levels. Through the use of a data-analysis protocol, team members were able to efficiently identify what the current reality was, what it might mean, and what they needed to do about it.

Their dialogue was rich, meaningful, and focused on what students were demonstrating when presenting written responses. The seventh-grade teachers found thirty-five students had improved significantly, the eighth-grade teacher found ten students had improved, the ninth-grade teachers identified twenty-seven who had improved, and the tenth-grade teachers identified thirteen students who had progressed well. This gave the team an idea of how it was tracking toward the achievement of its SMART goal.

It was clear that some of the practices and strategies that team members had been trialing were making a difference to their students' written responses; however, the analysis also revealed that some teachers were having more success than others in moving students along the scale. These discoveries lent themselves to further investigation.

With this in mind, the team then started to address a central question: Which instructional practices have led to higher levels of student success? Through this exploration, teachers were able to discuss their practices in more depth and identified the following two causal links.

1. Providing clear criteria when asking students to write a response during reflection time worked well.

2. Communicating looser explanations and expectations to students in reflection time resulted in the impact being less notable.

It became apparent that just having students write more, especially at the end of the lesson, was not enough to sustain improvement. The team also discovered that the teachers who made the greatest impact were more explicit in their expectations for written responses and shared simple scaffolds with which students could structure their writing. For example, the most successful practice was providing students with the following prompt.

Write down:

- Three things that you understand deeply as a result of the lesson
- Two things that are still murky for you
- One thing that you still struggle greatly with

This practice also required students to write their responses in full sentences and was always modeled by the teacher after asking students for their thoughts. The team discovered that strategies such as this one would be fairly simple to implement and trial in every member's classroom, and each made a commitment to do so.

The team also checked on its progress toward achieving its SMART goal and determined that a significant number of students had moved to the standard or above as a result of spending more time focusing on written responses in the classroom. Immersing the students in writing exercises was working, but team members felt there was still some way to go to meet their SMART goal. They decided to allow another six weeks before administering the final assessment, a fifteen-minute written response that they had identified at the beginning of the process.

Reviewing the Inquiry

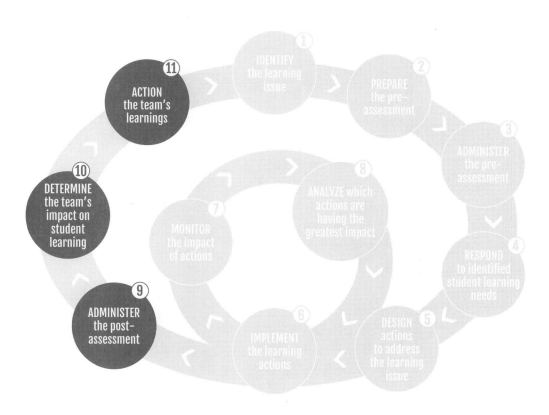

Action 9
Administer the Postassessment

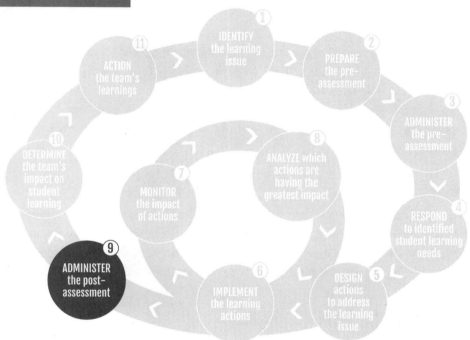

The Tasks

- Administer the end-of-cycle data-collection tool when quick checks show the team is close to achieving its SMART goal.

Once it becomes apparent the SMART goal has been achieved or is very close to being achieved, it is time to implement the data-collection tool or postassessment identified or developed in Action 2 (page 99). Though it isn't ideal, some teams may be required to undertake this action before having achieved the level of success initially hoped for due to time constraints and needing to move on to another learning issue in line with their school's strategic plan.

Before administering the postassessment, it is imperative that teams check that they have agreement on the method they will use to safeguard the fairness, validity, and reliability of the learning data they will gather.

In the Field

Elementary

At their meeting during week fourteen of semester two, the team members analyzed the data that they had continued to collect as they implemented the agreed strategies in their specialist subjects. This quick check data revealed that the team was close to achieving its SMART goal.

Finding themselves ahead of schedule, the members agreed to alter their original timeline and decided to reschedule the implementation of the postassessment for the following week. The team members reviewed the notes regarding the way that the data-collection tool would be implemented, which they had previously recorded in their meeting minutes. This ensured that all teachers implemented the postassessment in the agreed way.

Secondary

Six weeks after the previous meeting, the team administered the postassessment task. While the topic was different, the team ensured that the design of the assessment was the same as the one administered at the beginning of the cycle of learning, and members committed to comparing the resulting data to the baseline data at the next meeting.

Action 10
Determine the Team's Impact on Student Learning

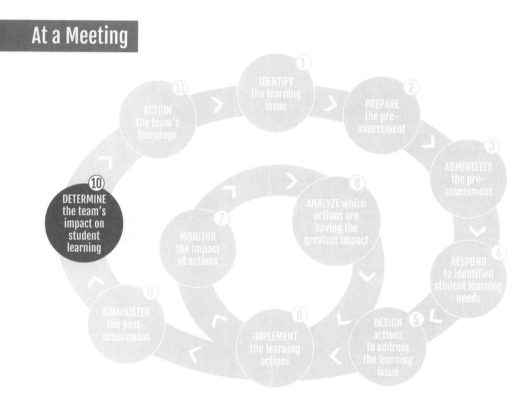

The Tasks

- Analyze the data to establish whether the team has achieved its SMART goal.

- Decide to continue, conclude, or postpone and return later to the cycle of learning.

- Celebrate informally individual and collective success in overcoming the identified learning issue.

Through analyzing and discussing the collected evidence of impact, teams have a genuine way to monitor and celebrate their success in addressing the learning issue that underpins a cycle of learning.

The data collected allow team members to determine their progress toward achieving the SMART goal set earlier in Action 4 of the cycle of learning process (page 105). Analysis of these data allows teams to make an informed decision as to whether to continue, conclude, or postpone and return later to the cycle of learning.

If an inquiry is not bound by specific time restrictions, the team conducting it might extend the cycle of learning if it hasn't achieved its SMART goal. This would be an appropriate response if a team has determined that it requires further time to embed successful actions into classroom practice before its SMART goal can be achieved.

Similarly, if a team discovers that it is well short of achieving its SMART goal, the team members might decide to postpone the cycle of learning as they undertake further discussion with one another to ensure that they implemented the chosen practices and strategies with fidelity. As a consequence of these discussions, they might decide they need to undertake further research to identify alternative practices that may have a greater impact on the identified learning issue.

Just as the celebration of progress is essential for students, the celebration of the individual and collective achievements of team members is vital. These celebrations remind teachers of the purpose and priorities of their daily work and motivate them in their continued endeavors. This is a crucial commitment in a school's journey to become an authentic, high-performing PLC. It can also serve as a reminder to teachers to celebrate the successes of their work with their students back in the classroom.

In the Field

Elementary

At the meeting scheduled after the implementation of the postassessment, the team reviewed the data that had been collected, calculated the average time lost, and compared what had been achieved to the SMART goal. The team members determined that the average time lost per specialist class following a break had been reduced to three minutes, meaning they had surpassed their original SMART goal of six minutes. They celebrated their achievements and planned how they would celebrate with their students.

When they reviewed each individual teacher's data, they noticed that one teacher had improved more than the others, reducing her average time lost by twenty minutes, from twenty-five minutes to just five minutes. This teacher was singled out for particular celebration and recognition from other team members.

Secondary

During their next meeting, team members were elated to see the progress so many students had made. The team had aimed for a 25 percent increase in students at standard or above on the end-of-year report. Plotted on the scale developed at the start of the cycle of learning, students had achieved an increase of 85 percent. Progress toward the SMART goal was tracking well, but a final determination could only be made when the end-of-year reports were finalized.

Reflecting on the impact of their actions across the cycle of learning, team members saw that the practices they implemented in their classrooms were making a genuine difference to their students' love of learning in science. The positive results also encouraged more reluctant team members to see the value of collaboratively addressing a learning issue.

Action 11
Action the Team's Learnings

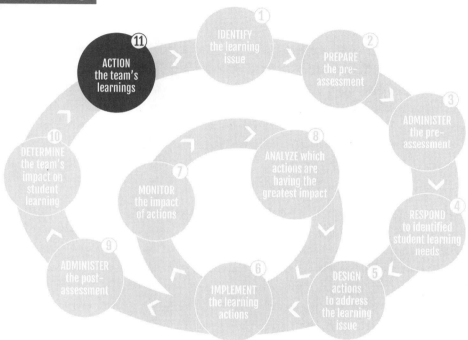

The Tasks

- Discuss what the team has learned through the cycle of learning, including identifying the most effective actions undertaken.
- Celebrate formally individual and collective growth in effectively modifying existing practices to address the learning issue.
- Embed the most successful actions into team members' individual and collective practice.
- Share the outcomes of the cycle of learning with other educators.

Transference of learning sits at the heart of actioning a team's learnings. This action requires teams to take everything they learned during a cycle of learning and apply it

137

to their future practices, programs, or approaches. What a team or school actually does with what it has learned has the potential to change its culture and shift its focus from teaching to learning.

The first task associated with actioning a team's learnings is spending time in a collaborative team meeting discussing what the team learned as a direct result of working through the cycle of learning. Using protocols to keep conversations focused and disciplined, teams must identify the practices that led to higher levels of learning for students. It is important to note that these learnings may relate to changes in instructional practices, team approaches, or the actual working of the collaborative team itself.

After recognizing what worked, teams can formalize the process of celebrating their success, which they will have commenced in the previous action (page 133). With the hectic pace of school life, this is a critical step to ensure educators feel satisfied with the difference they have made and help them maintain their motivation to continue to work collaboratively. Celebrations can be low-key affairs, with staff simply identifying successes and what led to them during a meeting, but there may also be more public recognition such as in newsletters, meeting minutes, emails, announcements on bulletin boards, staff meetings, or peer-recognition awards. Formalizing celebration in this way can provide the opportunity for other educators to learn from a team's action research, strengthening student learning across their school.

The most important consideration for a team at this stage of the cycle of learning is what it does with its learnings. This relates to transference and involves educators discussing, planning, and committing to changing their teaching practice as a result of what they have learned. They should also investigate ways of incorporating successful practices into other areas of their work, both individually and collectively. This stage also includes determining whether a learning issue warrants further investigation in another cycle of learning or if it has revealed another, more urgent learning issue worth addressing.

Finally, collaborative teams must find ways to share their learnings with their colleagues to ensure their work influences teaching practice beyond their own team. This can be an opportunity for school leaders to explore how the learnings of one team might benefit other teams' or whole-school practices, fostering a culture of job-embedded learning and continued school improvement.

In the Field

Elementary

At their next meeting, the team members reviewed what they had learned through the cycle of learning, determining which strategies should be adopted across all specialist areas. They decided that the car-parking system would become a permanent part of the entire team's teaching practice in all classes, not just those following a break. Three other strategies also proved to have a high impact and were justly incorporated into the specialist teachers' agreed pedagogy.

As the school's principal had shown interest in the team's investigation and had commented on how settled students now seemed in specialist programs, the team facilitator invited the principal to attend the meeting. The team used this opportunity to specifically recognize and celebrate the work of the team member whose results had shown the most improvement, who also happened to be a graduate teacher. The presence of the principal increased the importance of this celebration.

While the principal was present, the team outlined the major findings from the cycle of learning and detailed how the specialist teachers were going to modify their teaching approaches based on what they had learned. The team members also negotiated a time with the principal for when they could report back to the rest of the staff. They realized that the impactful strategies that they had identified through their action research would be useful for other teachers who often complained of a similar issue.

Secondary

In a meeting designed to capture the learnings of their action research, team members articulated what they had learned as a direct result of addressing the learning issue.

- Students need more time to write if they are going to improve their writing.
- It is up to teachers to prioritize that time.
- It isn't enough to just give students time to write; they also need simple directions and scaffolds to support them to be successful.
- Students need help to understand the explicit links between the written responses composed in the classroom and those composed as part of assessment tasks so they don't see them as separate things.

However, not only had they significantly increased their understanding of how to improve students' written responses in science they also identified that there had been a genuine increase in team members' collaborative engagement and ability to have focused discussions at team meetings as a consequence of the process. Team members also knew that they could apply what they had learned to other subjects they were teaching. In fact, many already were.

The ultimate celebration for this team came when the end-of-year reports showed monumental growth in student achievement in all areas of science. The team members could see the link between their actions in their classrooms to improve the quality of written responses and the increase in achievement as indicated by the common assessment tasks they administered. These improved scores contributed to the overall improvement displayed on students' final reports. They had moved 143 students to proficiency or above, well above the 125 students outlined in their SMART goal.

As a result of their success, their school's leadership team asked the science team to share what it had learned with other staff to improve students' written responses in other subject areas. The team chose to share these learnings in a practical way and focused on the difference the investigation had made to both student and teacher learning.

SECTION 5
Putting It All Together

Develop the Collaborative Team Meeting Agenda

We fully understand that educators are time poor and constantly being asked to perform additional tasks and take on additional responsibilities that distance them from tasks associated with improving student learning. We are also realists and understand that educators are unlikely to be given additional time to complete these tasks (although we view trying to increase collaborative team time as an essential task for school leaders). It is therefore imperative that collaborative teams repurpose their meeting time to focus on the right work and maximize the impact of the time that they *do* have to work together.

A clearly designed, targeted, and logically constructed meeting agenda is one critical way of ensuring that collaborative teams use their meeting time effectively and purposefully. In the initial stages of implementing the cycle of learning process, most teams will undertake a cycle as they learn the process and develop the skills required to implement it effectively. As team members' understanding and skills increase, they will quickly move on to concurrently implementing several cycles of learning in different curriculum areas or grade levels. Depending on the complexity of the skills, knowledge, and dispositions that are the focus of each cycle of learning, collaborative teams may find themselves at different points in cycles of learning being implemented simultaneously. Having a clear meeting agenda will support collaborative teams to implement each cycle with rigor and fidelity in an ordered and logical manner.

Through our work with schools, we have been able to develop, trial, and modify agenda formats for collaborative team meetings. We explore what we've learned here and include a sample template in appendix B (page 171) to support and assist teams in managing various tasks as they start to implement the cycle of learning process and build their capability to carry out the process with greater understanding and clarity.

We share this template as a possible starting point and encourage teams to adapt it to suit their own context and needs so they learn by doing. There are some key non-negotiable elements that must be included in any collaborative team meeting agenda to support the team in making its collective endeavors as purposeful and effective as possible.

Team Norms

Norms are essentially a team's rules of engagement and should detail the behaviors that all team members agree to hold themselves to at meetings. We strongly recommend that meeting agendas include a list of previously developed team norms in a prominent position. This ensures that a team's collective behavioral commitments remain at the fore during each meeting and can be quickly referred to and referenced if required.

As norms should be detailed as clearly as possible and take in the key areas of time, decision making, participation, listening, confidentiality, and expectations, it may not be possible to fit a complete list of all team norms within each meeting agenda. Instead, we encourage teams to include a short, concise list of their agreed-on common beliefs around each of these areas in their agenda, while listing the specific behaviors that they have agreed to demonstrate at meetings in a supplementary document of norms. In some schools we have worked with, each team's full documentation of norms is housed in a plastic holder that is placed on the table at the start of meetings. This serves as a reminder of the complete version of their agreed norms and supports team members to transition to the meeting expectations. For example, a team might agree on the following norm.

It is vital to use meeting time effectively and productively at all times.

This norm belief for time would then be recorded on the agenda. Unpacking how they can support this belief, team members might then agree to demonstrate the following specific behaviors.

- We will arrive at meetings on time.
- We will conclude meetings at the scheduled time unless all team members agree to an extension.
- We will have carried out all actions as decided at the previous meeting.
- We will collaboratively agree to the time spent on all agenda items.
- We will park issues that arise during the meeting when necessary and return to them at an appropriate time.
- We will bring all required items to the meeting.

These more specific behaviors that support the norm belief should then be recorded in the team's fuller norm documentation.

One of the common things that we have observed during our work with schools is the quick initial uptake and acceptance of the need for meeting norms. We believe that there are two main reasons for this. The first is that articulating norms is a tangible and relatively simple task that schools and teams can undertake to commence their school's transformation into a PLC. Second, many schools and teams have struggled with the diversity of opinions and beliefs that educators bring to the table when they meet, and introducing norms seems like a simple solution. However, though many schools we have worked with embrace the idea to begin with, often on subsequent visits we find that all reference to meeting norms will have disappeared. When queried, teams typically inform us that they haven't had the need to refer to or use their norms or agreed-on breach procedures. This is a strong indication that the school or team hasn't yet shifted its focus and attention to the real work of a collaborative team in a PLC.

When teams start to implement the cycle of learning process and discussions are centered more rigorously on improving student learning and identifying which teaching practices are having the greatest impact, the need for norms will be heightened. If team members don't feel safe or trust their colleagues, they will not make themselves vulnerable and will not seek advice when their students aren't reaching the desired level. They will be reluctant to reveal any weakness in their teaching practice. Listing agreed norms—or at least norm beliefs—on each agenda is a way of countering this reluctance and keeping agreed behavior commitments at the front of team members' minds, particularly when the depth of discussions and need for professional disagreement increase.

Norm-Breach Procedure

The norm-development process should occur when a team first meets at the commencement of a school year (or when a team is first formed) and should also involve the development of a procedure for when these norms are breached. Being pre-emptive and knowing that norms are there to support the work of the team, each team should anticipate that at some point norms will be broken. To ensure norm breaches are dealt with in a professional manner, teams should develop an agreed-on approach to address them. This is critical because one of the most difficult things for educators to do is professionally challenge the behaviors of their colleagues in a way that keeps student learning at the core of their collaborative work.

The development of this process should involve team members considering how they would like to be treated if they happen to break a norm. The result should be a tiered response in which the severity of the action taken increases if a person continues to breach his or her team's agreed-on behavioral norms. For example, a team's agreed-on response to a norm breach might be a team member tapping the table twice. If this action doesn't solve the norm breach, the next tier of response might be for the matter to be added as an item to discuss at the following meeting.

Once agreement has been reached on a team's norm-breach procedure, there is value in summarizing this in its meeting agenda. Doing so reminds team members of the commitment they have given to adhering to the established norms and cautions them of the process that will be followed when breaches occur.

Team Roles

Over time, it is important to build team members' abilities to fully support the successful functioning of meeting processes. As such, there is great value in having specific rotating roles for team members at meetings. This process not only ensures all members contribute to the effectiveness of the meeting but also supports the distributive leadership practices of high-performing PLCs.

Many teams will have a nominated team leader who supports the team and provides a link to school leadership. However, it is important that this leader isn't seen as the person who makes all the decisions or directs his or her team's thinking. At the team meeting, this person's role is more as a facilitator than the ultimate decision maker.

This person might be involved in preparing the processes and protocols his or her team will use at meetings to ensure in-depth discussions and decisions that focus on improving student learning. This doesn't necessarily mean that this person has to then chair every meeting. As the strengths of team members develop, others might chair meetings with the team leader simply acting as a guide by their side. Some common roles that many collaborative teams use at meetings are chairperson, minute-taker, norm-observer (also known as *critical friend*), and timekeeper.

We have included space in the sample agenda template (appendix B, page 171) so the names of team members fulfilling these roles can be recorded.

Critical PLC Questions

Sometimes teams mistakenly adopt the critical PLC questions as agenda items for their meetings. This gives the false impression that all of the critical questions can be addressed at every collaborative team meeting.

As can be seen in the tasks to be undertaken in meetings throughout the process, these questions weave their way through teams' collaborative endeavors with each attracting emphasis and focus on different phases in a cycle of learning. Teams shouldn't focus their meetings on trying to answer these questions. Rather, the outcome of doing the right work is that these questions will be answered.

Though they are not agenda items, listing the critical questions at the top of the meeting agenda template reminds teams of what they are trying to address through the work they do. They act as a filter to deprioritize or remove tasks that do not support their resolution. The actual agenda items for each meeting must be determined by the tasks to be undertaken as the various actions in a cycle of learning are carried out.

Learning Focus Items

We split the rest of the agenda into three distinct sections, the first of which is reserved for the discussion of what we call *learning focus items*. These items correlate to the various actions and associated tasks of the cycle of learning process that need to be scheduled at collaborative team meetings so that teams can hold discussions and reach agreement. Learning focus items should be the foremost focus of collaborative team meetings and be allocated the greatest amount of time.

We suggest using three columns for each agenda item: (1) Item, (2) Time Allocation, and (3) Decisions. These columns allow teams to outline the agenda item, record the estimated time that the team will devote to the item, and note the major actions and agreements that the team reaches as a result of its discussions.

Item

This column allows teams to clearly itemize the agenda so that all members understand the points that need to be addressed. It is also important that all collaborative team members understand the purpose of each agenda item so that their discussions (and the actions they develop as a consequence of these discussions) are aligned to what the team hopes to achieve by the tabling of the item.

As such, we recommended that when each item is introduced, the desired outcomes and a guiding question are also clearly articulated. This will ensure that the discussions are more focused and move the team forward to achieve an outcome. For example, the desired outcome of an item tabled as "Develop the preassessment" might be articulated as follows.

> *By the end of our discussion of this item, we want to have created a think map with assessment tasks that clearly align to the six specific skills we are targeting through this cycle of learning. We also will have agreed on the answers we will accept as correct and on the proforma sheet we will use to collate the data we collect.*

This practice ensures that all team members have clarity regarding what the team will achieve as a result of the agenda item. A question to guide this item of inquiry might be something like the following.

> *What might the students need to demonstrate to us that will inform what is included on the think map?*

By including an open question like this for each agenda item, teams can create the conditions for genuine collaborative inquiry and focused problem solving.

Meeting time will become increasingly precious as the cycle of learning progresses. This means teams need to make sure they use every second purposely and productively to get the right work done at the meeting, or risk having to complete it at another time.

Time Allocation

As meeting time is precious, it is important that all items have a suggested amount of time allocated to them. This will ensure that meetings don't run overtime and discussions don't become unfocused or lack informed decision making. A team's facilitator might take on the role of allocating suggested times to agenda items initially, but with practice and understanding, involving team members in this task ensures greater commitment to specific time allocations and understanding of why they are necessary.

At the start of each agenda item, the person allocated the timekeeping role in a meeting should remind all present of the time that has been allocated to the item. At key points, particularly for longer agenda items, the timekeeper should also remind team members of the time remaining. This ensures that the discussion moves forward toward agreement on an action to be taken. A timekeeper may also ask his or her team to consider whether the time allocated for an agenda item needs to be extended. For example, "We have five minutes left. Do you think that we can reach agreement on the actions we need to take as a consequence of this discussion, or do we need to extend the time?" If an extension is necessary, then team members should adjust the time allowed on an upcoming item or items so that the meeting still finishes on time.

We have found that as teams become more familiar with managing the tasks associated with the cycle of learning process, they develop the skills to use the time allocated to agenda items with greater flexibility and with less regimentation. Team members should remember that the allocation of time is a best guess and not necessarily set in stone. The last thing we want is for collaborative team members to artificially curtail their discussion and collective problem solving and make a less-informed and considered decision just to meet the suggested time allocation. As team members gain experience, they will be able to use the suggested time wisely as a way of ensuring discussions are solution and action focused, rather than seeing the aim as rigidly adhering to the exact second of the time allocated for each agenda item.

Decisions

The third and final column is designed for a meeting's minute-taker to record the main actions or outcomes that his or her team agrees to take as a result of its discussion of an agenda item.

Minute-takers sometimes try, for accountability reasons, to record the whole narrative of the discussion that the team undertakes to agree on decisions or actions. While recording some of the major points might be beneficial, a full recording of the narrative is not. When this is attempted, the minute-taker's input into discussion is limited or nonexistent.

At key points in discussions, it is beneficial to have someone (this might be the job of the chairperson, timekeeper, or minute-taker) prompt the team by asking questions. For example, "Given what we have discussed, what are the actions we are agreeing to take?" This ensures that collaborative problem solving and decision making are always the outcome. Prompting and questioning in this way support team members to reach agreement on what they are committing to as a result of their discussion. By doing this regularly, team members will be reminded that the power of their collaborative discussions and problem solving is in the actions they agree to take outside their meetings. These agreements or actions should then be recorded in this third column.

It is important that each discussion reaches a definitive and clear conclusion so that everyone knows what they need to do as a result. Good practice is for team facilitators to summarize each discussion and confirm the decisions reached at the end of each agenda item. For example, "It sounds like, as a result of everyone having their say, the suggestion is to implement an 'exit-pass' system with all our students by the end of week eight and to bring the corrected results with us for discussion in the next meeting. Is everyone in agreement with this?" It is important that everyone is clear about any proposed action and feels that they have had input into the discussions that generate decisions. This builds accountability to follow through on agreed actions and collective decisions.

Standing Items for the Start and End of Each Meeting

There are several mandatory agenda items that should appear at the start and end of each meeting. These items are *standing items* and focus on building each collaborative team member's skills and practices. They also build a level of accountability into the decisions agreed to by team members.

The collaborative team meeting is the "engine room" of school improvement. Continuous school improvement is built on the premise of the unrelenting strengthening of educators' capabilities. This enables them to implement the cycle of learning process with fidelity and ever-increasing levels of accomplishment. If, after using the process for several years, a collaborative team is implementing cycles of learning with the same level of success as when it started, its attempts to use collaborative team meetings as forums for continued school improvement has, at best, stalled—at worst, failed.

We have found that including these standing items enhances clarity, efficiency, commitment, productivity, and a sense of shared ownership. Given that improving student learning depends on the output of a team's collective endeavors, it is critical that these standing items are included on every collaborative team meeting agenda.

Start: Establish a Focus Norm

The aim of each meeting is twofold: (1) to focus team members' endeavors on the right work and (2) to increase their capabilities to do this work. Each meeting carried out by a team should have a *focus norm* designed to strengthen the team's skills in working together at increasingly higher levels of disciplined collaboration, as well as a designated norm-observer (or critical friend) to provide feedback at the meeting's conclusion. The focus norm selected for a meeting should be directly related to improving an aspect of collaborative practice identified at the previous meeting.

After opening a meeting, a team facilitator might state something like the following.

> *At our last meeting, our norm-observer noted that we struggled with talking over each other in our enthusiasm to share our ideas. I'm going to give everyone thirty seconds to quickly jot down actions you are personally going to take to ensure that this doesn't also happen at today's meeting.*

Whether or not they decide to share these actions, the result is that all team members will be reminded of the focus norm and have the opportunity to think about how they will ensure they won't breach the norm at the current meeting.

The aim of this process is to socialize the idea of adhering to norms, allowing each team member the opportunity to develop his or her individual and collective capabilities to enhance the overall effectiveness of the team. Norms are living commitments. Additional norms can be added as new, nonproductive meeting behaviors surface. For example, a norm-observer might report at the end of a meeting that at several times team members started to discuss issues that were unrelated to the agenda item. This might lead the team's facilitator to start the next meeting with a related reflection, as in the following example.

> *At our last meeting, our norm-observer noted that we were tending to engage in topics unrelated to the matter being discussed. What is a norm we could create to ensure this behavior doesn't impact the important work we have to do as a team?*

The team would then discuss and develop an appropriate new norm to add to its existing norms and focus on it until the counterproductive behavior has been remedied.

Start: Review the Actions Agreed to at the Last Meeting

The next standing item at the start of the meeting agenda should be a quick review of the agreed-on actions or decisions from the previous meeting. By including this item, team members know they will be held accountable for implementing the agreed-on actions and decisions. If responsibility has been delegated to a specific team member or several team members, they are required to provide a quick report on their endeavors.

End: Allocate Roles for the Next Meeting

We strongly recommended that the roles team members will take at each meeting are clearly communicated and collaboratively agreed to at the meeting prior. This ensures each team member understands what is expected of him or her both during and in preparation for a meeting, and minimizes time wasting.

Should anyone have any questions or uncertainties about his or her upcoming role, these can be addressed and followed up outside meeting time with the appropriate person (this is usually the team facilitator or the team member who held the role in question at the most recent meeting).

End: Develop Items for the Next Meeting's Agenda

The development of agenda items for collaborative team meetings should be the responsibility of all team members and take place in the meeting prior. However, when team members are learning and becoming more familiar with the cycle of learning process, a team's leader or facilitator might offer greater guidance and direction. Where this is the case, there is still merit in developing agendas together as a team, as this allows the team facilitator to articulate why certain items are being included and assists other team members to become more familiar with the cycle of learning process.

Developing the next meeting's agenda at the end of each meeting guarantees that agendas eventually become the responsibility of the whole team and not just that of a team facilitator. It also means that this task is at least started during meetings and doesn't become another job for someone to attend to in his or her own time.

As we have detailed in this book, there is a chronological order to the various actions and tasks in a cycle of learning. Many agenda items for the next meeting will be a consequence of the actions and tasks undertaken at or as a result of a current team meeting, making the agenda development process meaningful and logical for all involved.

End: Review the Decisions Made in the Meeting

To enable clarity and strengthen accountability, a quick recap of all agreed actions or decisions made by a team should conclude each meeting. This review confirms that all team members are clear on the actions or decisions they are required to follow up.

This could be the task of the minute-taker and might sound something like, "Here are the actions that I think we agreed to at this meeting. As I read them back, can you check I have recorded these correctly and if they need further clarification?" After reading each decision, the minute-taker might ask, "Have I recorded that correctly? Is everyone clear on what we have committed to?" If any actions have established timelines or are the responsibility of specific team members, these should be clarified similarly. There can be no excuses then as to why an action hasn't been taken or followed up.

Ensure that near the start of the following meeting, time is allocated to reflect on the actions from the previous meeting. This is when members with specific responsibilities as agreed in the meeting prior should report back on the results of the actions they were required to take.

End: Review the Focus Norm

At the end of each meeting, the norm-observer should provide feedback on how the team's behaviors helped to strengthen its practices in the focus area. This final concluding item on the agenda is complementary to the establishment of a focus norm at the start of each meeting and might have the norm-observer respond to the following prompt questions, which should also focus his or her observations over the course of the meeting.

- How purposeful and effective were we as a collaborative team at this meeting?
- What behaviors or issues impacted how effective and efficient we were in doing the work we undertook at this meeting?
- What specific evidence of behaviors supports this judgment?

The norm-observer should report back on the team's effectiveness, relating his or her evaluation specifically to articulated norms. For example, a norm-observer might conclude a meeting with the following statement.

> At this meeting, we did really well at analyzing the learning data. Team members came to the meeting having reviewed the data in their own time, which allowed us to move straight into a discussion of the actions we were going to take in response to the data. I did notice, however, when we were brainstorming actions we are going to trial back in our classrooms, that we all become a bit overzealous and were cutting one another off before the person speaking had the opportunity to explain their ideas fully.

In this reflection, a norm-observer should also provide specific examples of behaviors that he or she witnessed to justify his or her opinion and feedback. It is important that this evidence does not specifically identify individual team members. As much as possible, feedback should be related to collective team behaviors with the genuine desire to continually increase a team's collective effectiveness and purposefulness. Depending on the amount of time available, team members may be asked to respond to the norm-observer's feedback or reflect on the list of personal behaviors they jotted down at the start of the meeting, which they might then share in the form of a quick review: "I contributed to the meeting of this norm by . . . ."

If it is felt that the team has improved in their focus area, a different focus norm can then be selected for the following meeting. If the team decides that the issue hasn't been resolved, the focus norm might carry over through several meetings until members observe adequate and consistent improvement.

Minute-takers should also make note in the meeting minutes of any norms their team struggled with. This norm-reflection stage must be a team's genuine attempt to continue to refine its collaborative practices and skills. The practice refines the quality of the work that members undertake and increases the impact that they are able to have on student learning. Meetings may conclude after this standing item has been addressed.

Scheduling these reviews as standing items at the beginning and end of each meeting ensures that there is no confusion or uncertainty about the outcomes of any meeting, and team members are able to commit to following through on agreed actions or decisions as required. It also ensures that neither item can be accidentally skipped or overlooked, further strengthening accountability because those required to take action will have clarity about what they must do and understand that they will also be required to report back to their team.

Administrative Items

There should also be a separate section of the agenda for administrative items. These items should have a limited amount of time allocated to them at collaborative team meetings.

All collaborative teams have other responsibilities and functions that are expedient to carry out when the team comes together. As they are typically less complex and challenging than the actions and tasks associated with cycles of learning, focusing on administrative or communication-based items can give teams a false sense of achievement as a result of being able to cross things off their to-do list. While these tasks are important, teams that understand what their real work is limit the intrusion of administrative items on valuable meeting time. This is to ensure adequate time for the actions and tasks more directly aligned with maximizing continued student learning.

To cater for administrative items, a specific section should be included on meeting agendas where these items can be dealt with separate from learning focus items. It is vital that these items have a short and specified time allocated to them and that the outcomes from these items are captured in meeting minutes.

In some high-performing collaborative teams, this section of the agenda is removed from the collaborative team meeting completely so that the items don't take up precious and limited meeting time. Instead, these administrative tasks are dealt with during a shorter meeting held at another time so that a clear distinction is maintained between the two sets of tasks and their purposes.

When schools begin their transformation into a PLC, it is important that they undertake a review of the communication strategies used within the school to keep staff informed of vital information. Schools are complex organizations with a large amount of information that needs to be shared to support their smooth running and daily operations. Both general staff meetings and collaborative team meetings are convenient forums for this information to be relayed, but this then reduces valuable time that could be used more purposefully to advance their school's quest to improve student learning. Schools benefit from auditing the amount of valuable meeting time lost in this way so they can then make informed decisions about how best to minimize their ongoing impact.

Read-Only Items

This section of the collaborative team agenda is, as the name implies, for communicating information that doesn't need any discussion or elaboration, as listed items are merely reminders of things that team members need to be aware of. The responsibility for listing these lies with members who have information to share. Collaborative teams will often create their meeting agendas and minutes on a shared platform that allows all members to contribute. This allows team members and school leaders to add items to the document for others to access and read at any time.

When adding an item, team members should also list their name so that if anyone requires any further clarification or information, he or she can approach them directly outside the meeting, as in the following example.

> *The new books for the upcoming science unit of work have been purchased and are currently being processed by the library. These will be available for team members to borrow from the beginning of the fifth week of this semester. —Peter A.*

Often team members are concerned that communication items might not be read and acted on by others if a verbal reminder is not given in their meetings, even if it's present on the agenda. However, acting on read-only items is a professional expectation and responsibility of all team members. If this becomes an issue, team members must review the impact it is having and in response, come up with a norm to add to their existing list.

Upcoming Events

The final section should include a weekly calendar for the term. While many schools have detailed electronic or written calendars that detail the weekly, semester-based, and yearly events for school personnel, this calendar serves a different purpose. It allows teams to schedule tasks for cycles of learning and record events that might impact implementation.

For example, a team might record that students will be on camp in week five and, therefore, that week's collaborative team meeting will not be held. As the team meets in the weeks prior to the camp, the meeting that will be missed can be specifically accommodated for. Similarly, a team might schedule postassessment for week nine. This could be added to the team's calendar so that team members have a visual reminder of this in meetings held in the preceding weeks.

Strategies for Making the Agenda Work

As we have highlighted, true collaborative teams that work within a PLC are problem-solving teams. We've offered this exploration of the key components of a highly successful collaborative team's meeting agenda, as well as a meeting agenda template in appendix B (page 171) as possible starting points for teams just beginning to implement the cycle of learning. We actively encourage high-performing collaborative teams to adapt, modify, and review their agenda format and meeting structure so that they meet the team's unique context and circumstances. When team members innovate and enhance their agenda format, they transform from a group of people working together into a collaborative team that works.

Highly productive teams employ strategies like the following to ensure their ongoing collaborative efforts are both impactful and efficient.

Working in Subteams

In larger collaborative teams, at certain phases of the cycle of learning process, tasks may be delegated at meetings to smaller *subteams* for greater time efficiency or to allow a higher level of involvement and input from team members.

If this occurs, it is important that time is allocated for each subteam to report back to the whole team within the meeting. This allows team members working in other subteams to develop an understanding of what their colleagues have been working on. It allows questions to be asked and clarification to be sought so that the work of each subteam is owned and committed to by the entire team.

If a subteam has not completed its assigned task, its members should use this time as an opportunity to outline an action plan with other team members for the task to be completed. This would then inform the team's agenda for its next meeting.

Parking Items

No matter how disciplined or experienced a team is, at some point discussions will veer off topic and into areas far removed from stated agenda items. If discussions do start to drift to side issues or take unimportant detours, it is crucial to address these so that valuable meeting time is not lost.

A possible way of doing this is by introducing a *parking system* for these topics. If a team member thinks of something he or she feels is important while the team is discussing other issues, have this member "park" the idea by recording it on a sticky note so it isn't lost. Team members can do this independently, but others might also prompt this action if they notice the discussion getting sidetracked with a comment such as this: "That's an important issue. Note it down, and we will come back to it when we have finished with the items on the agenda."

This approach allows the discussion to continue without it moving into a noncritical area, ensuring that the focus remains on achieving the desired outcome or completing the task. If issues, topics, or thoughts are parked in this way, it is important that the team comes back to them, either at the end of the meeting if time allows for whole-team discussion or at another appropriate time for a more personal follow-up.

Building Team Facilitators' Capabilities

Team facilitators require professional learning support during the early stages of implementing the cycle of learning process. This is primarily to assist them in understanding the importance of the processes and protocols associated with their collaborative team's work. School leaders play an important role in expanding the capacity of team facilitators to support the ongoing work of collaborative teams. Once team facilitators gain clarity and confidence in the cycle of learning process, they can continue to learn by doing.

As team facilitators start to learn by doing, school leaders should implement ways for them to share the good practices, processes, and protocols being developed and used within their collaborative team meetings with other facilitators. By providing opportunities for team facilitators to share their successes, leaders can extend and enhance their school's collaborative practices. Areas that team facilitators identify that they or their teams are struggling with must then become the focus of continued professional learning and problem solving with the support of their leadership team.

School leaders are the conduit for collective inquiry and action research in support of their school's continued PLC journey. The focus and work of the school leaders must be action research into how they can continue to transform their school into a high-performing PLC. Supporting team facilitators to develop their identities, knowledge, skills, and aptitude is a non-negotiable element of leaders' responsibility to the process. Leaders also need to support facilitators to develop and use the protocols and artifacts, including strong meeting agendas, necessary to lead their collaborative teams. These are integral foundations on which future successes are built.

A Leadership Team's Responsibility for the Process

We define a *PLC* as the whole school, while collaborative teams are the engines of school improvement. A metaphor we often use when explaining the PLC process to schools is that of an orange. We ask participants in our workshops to consider the whole school to be the skin of the orange and collaborative teams as the segments. Without its protective skin, the orange segments dry up, go moldy, and eventually rot. Similarly, it is impossible for collaborative teams to perform the actions and attend to the tasks required to improve student learning if, at a whole-school level, the culture and structures don't exist to support their work. We have personally witnessed collaborative teams flounder and become ineffective when these crucial foundations have been absent.

This important aspect of being a PLC also was recognized by Marzano and his colleagues (2016) in *Collaborative Teams That Transform Schools* when they added another critical question to those put forward in the PLC at Work process: How do we coordinate our efforts as a school? This question asks leaders to consider how they ensure that the necessary whole-school conditions have been created to allow their collaborative teams to thrive. This question challenges leadership teams to think about not only the responsibilities of teams and the work that they have to do but also their own responsibility for supporting collaborative teams by fostering both the structures and learning-focused culture teams need to thrive.

In the PLC at Work process, DuFour and his coauthors (2016) stress the importance of building a supportive foundation to sustain the work of collaborative teams. In this process, a great deal of attention is given to creating a schoolwide culture that ensures collaborative teams can take action and engage in the work they need to undertake. According to DuFour and his colleagues (2016), the foundation of a successful PLC rests on four pillars: a school's (1) mission, (2) vision, (3) values, and (4) goals. Informed by the work of people such as Jim Collins (2001), these pillars provide the support necessary for a school's ongoing commitment to being a PLC. One of the reasons we are so committed to ensuring this part of the PLC at Work process is implemented with fidelity is because of the difficulties we have seen collaborative teams experience when these foundations are absent or only afforded scant attention.

To help build a safe and supportive culture that allows collaborative teams to take the actions required to achieve high levels of learning for all, we strongly advocate that schools are clear about their fundamental purpose or mission. All school personnel must also be united by a precise and compelling vision that describes what their school will be like when it is achieving high levels of learning for all. All staff need to be clear on the collective behavioral commitments required to work in a PLC and fully understand the goals that they are supporting the school to achieve through their collaborative endeavors. Attention also needs to be paid to the team structures that are established and how leadership responsibilities are distributed across a school.

School leaders must also consider the ways they can provide relentless and authentic support to their collaborative teams. They must act as exemplary models of the behavior they want staff to demonstrate as they go about their work. Other aspects that schools need to consider when building a safe and supportive culture are opportunities for cross-team collaboration, how improvements in adult and student learning can be genuinely celebrated, ways to ensure all teams adhere to norms, and how those in leadership positions can support educators in building the skills of productive collaboration.

In this section we outline the actions that school leadership teams can take as they create the necessary conditions for collaborative teams to implement the cycle of learning process.

Bring the School's Mission to Life

The power of a mission statement is not in the carefully crafted words written on paper but in the clarity it provides to galvanize and unite everyone around the school's fundamental purpose. A school needs to be united by a common mission that connects and compels all stakeholders toward the achievement of high levels of learning for all. In establishing this uniting vision, school leaders need to ensure staff have the opportunity to explore and inquire into current research regarding what improves student learning and what practices highly effective schools incorporate to improve teaching practice and student learning. In doing so, school leaders develop and strengthen their staff's collective efficacy and belief that their individual and collective endeavors can allow them to overcome all other factors that impact on student learning.

Through the process of developing a clear, succinct, and uniting school mission, all staff and stakeholders are actively encouraged to explore their current beliefs about the purpose of their school and their role in improving student learning. This leads to greater commitment from all staff to the fundamental purpose of their school. Once a clear mission has been established, it needs to be socialized to the point where it is clearly known by staff and key stakeholders so that they see the connection between it and their daily work. School leaders must continually involve staff in processes that ensure their mission becomes more than words on a piece of paper. A school's mission needs to be lived daily through the work of all stakeholders.

By constantly engaging staff in exploring what their mission means to their daily work, school leaders can ensure that any underlying beliefs that might jeopardize commitment are respectfully challenged and changed over time. Aligning their mission to their school's strategic and annual implementation plans, school leaders ensure that their mission statement can be translated into the manageable and tangible actions that underpin the ongoing work of their collaborative teams.

Create a School Vision Collaboratively

A measure of a strongly crafted and carefully composed vision statement is its power to reach through time and propel staff toward the future school they are trying to create.

Educators in a PLC need to understand what their school might be like when they are closer to achieving their mission so that they have a clear and united understanding of what they are working toward. We have supported schools to develop clear vision statements that focus on student learning, but it is essential that the generative process also involves staff and key stakeholders. This ensures collective ownership and develops a common understanding of how the ongoing work they do and the way they do it moves the school closer to achieving its mission.

As with its mission statement, a school's vision must be socialized to the point of being well known, with everyone understanding their personal role. This requires school leaders to ensure they establish an ongoing process that involves staff in the evaluation of their school's progress toward achieving its documented vision. Importantly, school leaders must also ensure that the vision they develop aligns with and drives their school's strategic and annual implementation plans. They must constantly articulate and clarify how the actions of all involved in implementing these plans contribute to their school's efforts to realize its vision.

Build Collective Commitments

School leaders must involve their staff in the development of collective commitments that clearly outline the expected behaviors required to move their school closer to achieving its mission and vision. These collective commitments, made to one another, describe how school personnel will behave to ensure high levels of student learning.

These collective commitments again must be socialized to a point where they are well known, adhered to, and ultimately embraced by all staff. When staff are clear on the behaviors required to work collaboratively and focus on the right work, they are in a much better position to learn and conduct collaborative inquiry together. The collective commitments outline the way they commit to work together to ensure their school's mission and vision are achieved.

It is often said that behavior ignored is behavior condoned. Part of the process of developing collective commitments, which should also involve all staff, is the development of breach procedures that outline the processes that teams will follow if collective commitments are violated. These procedures will change over time as school leaders monitor the effectiveness of processes and make necessary adjustments.

Staff must hold themselves accountable for adhering to the collective commitments they have been involved in creating and must also implement the agreed-on procedures when breaches to those commitments occur. Providing professional learning to staff to ensure that they feel comfortable in implementing agreed-on breach procedures is a key step in creating a school culture that focuses on working collaboratively and improving learning.

The development of collective commitments is key to ensuring staff have clarity on the behaviors that are required to achieve their school's mission and vision, and must be deliberately enacted through strategic plans. School leaders should also look for opportunities to discuss, monitor, review, and adjust their school's collective commitments. Highly effective school leaders use staff's demonstration of behaviors aligned to the agreed-on collective commitments as a way of monitoring their school's progress toward becoming a PLC.

Establish a Goal-Oriented Culture

Common goals are the glue that binds members of a PLC together. Without developing clearly articulated long-term and annual goals informed by relevant and contextual data in key areas, schools will ultimately fall short of improving student learning.

School leaders must ensure that collaborative teams are aware of their school's annual SMART goals and understand how the work of their teams contributes to the achievement of those overarching goals. They must also monitor and frequently share with staff the progress being made toward achieving these goals over the course of the school year. This allows both leaders and collaborative teams to make adjustments to their practices as necessary to meet the goals.

It is also important that schoolwide goals inform schools' strategic and annual implementation plans and are specific enough to focus all school personnel's endeavors on the key areas identified as having the greatest impact on improving student learning.

Form Teams That Maximize Impact on Learning

In forming collaborative teams, school leaders must ask, "Do team members have a shared responsibility for responding to issues around curriculum, assessment, and instruction in ways that enhance students' learning?" Whenever a leadership team is forming collaborative structures, student and teacher learning must always be placed at the heart of decision making. As we've highlighted, a key strength of the PLC at Work process is connection between members of a collaborative team as forged through the common content they deliver to their students.

Protect Time for Collaborative Team Meetings

Another important requirement to progress a school's journey to become a PLC is identifying when and how frequently collaborative teams will meet. In high-performing PLCs, school leaders establish a clear meeting schedule that allows collaborative teams to meet during the contractual school day. It would be disingenuous to recognize the important role that collaborative teams play in improving student learning and then ask educators to find time to meet outside of school hours. School leaders must instead prioritize allowing time for collaborative teams to meet, recognizing that this meeting time provides the greatest opportunity to improve student learning of all school meetings. They must also recognize the complexity of the work collaborative teams are required to undertake and appreciate that these tasks take time. Doing so lays the groundwork for collaborative teams to reach their true potential as the engines of school improvement, while establishing disorganized or inadequate meeting schedules is a sure way to undermine their endeavors before they even begin.

School leaders, through their monitoring and advocacy, must ensure that collaborative team meeting time is protected so that meetings occur regularly and without interruption, and also that collaborative team members are clear on the purpose of these meeting and the focus of their collaborative endeavors. This is to minimize the risk of the work of teams being compromised, left to chance, or governed by personal preference or the most dominant voice. School leaders understand that they will need to provide professional learning not only on the specific actions and tasks that collaborative teams will perform but also on the skills and processes necessary to work at high levels of collaboration. To assist in this, we've outlined some important skills of inquiry in appendix A (page 167).

Establish a Whole-School RTI

All successful RTI approaches must be coordinated across a whole school, mobilizing all available resources and personnel in the establishment of a multilayered system of support for students to achieve or exceed required learning standards.

It is essential that school leaders establish not only structures that allow time for collaborative teams to meet but also a whole-school RTI. Leaders of high-performing and impactful PLCs understand that without a rigorous and research-based whole-school approach to addressing student learning failure, collaborative teams' attempts to achieve high levels of learning for all will be severely compromised.

Expand Opportunities for Distributed Leadership

High-performing PLCs implement a distributed approach to leadership. Alma Harris (2014) advances that distributed leadership is primarily concerned with the practice of leadership rather than specific leadership roles or responsibilities. Through distributed leadership, schools maximize their capacity for change and improvement. By activating leadership expertise throughout a school, more opportunities are created to embed improvement endeavors. Distributed leadership builds the collaborative culture of a school, as interdependent interactions and practices become the norm. Marzano and his colleagues (2016) confirm that by flattening the organization of a school, leaders assist in its transformation into a PLC.

It is essential that school leaders develop their staff's understanding of their authority to make instructional decisions, provided they are unequivocally aligned to their school's mission, vision, and goals. As teams conduct action research and inquire into the teaching practices that have the greatest impact on student learning, it is vital that they have the freedom to actively explore and pursue promising practices. Top-down efforts to change teaching practice seldom work. However, when teams are invested in the outcomes of their inquiry and have the professional freedom to monitor their individual and collective impact on student learning, they are more likely to alter their teaching practices and get the results they desire.

To promote the distribution of leadership across their organization, school leaders should ensure that each team has a nominated team facilitator. These facilitators must then be assisted in their role through regular meetings with their school's formal leadership team, which provides ongoing support and professional learning to continually build the teams' capabilities to run highly impactful and focused team meetings. In the absence of this support, collaborative team leaders can often feel the overwhelming pressure, burden, and confusion of attempting to enact change without having clarity around what it is they are trying to implement or the necessary skills to do so.

In high-performing PLCs, there is a synergy across all levels of the school as a result of this distribution of leadership, and staff work collectively in support of one another to fulfill their school's mission and vision. A failure for one is seen as a failure for all, and is felt acutely by everyone.

Maximize Leadership Support

Leaders of successful PLCs continually align school resources, both human and otherwise, to ensure the achievement of school and team goals. On an ongoing basis, they monitor how the allocation of school resources is supporting the achievement of school and team goals, making adjustments to address any issues as they occur.

School leaders must also provide teams and facilitators access to research, templates, protocols, exemplars, and artifacts connected to the PLC process and collaborative teams to support their work. Working alongside team leaders, assisting them when they face challenges and uncertainties, school leaders must understand that their contribution to school improvement is measured through the direct support they give to collaborative teams as they go about their work. It is this continued support that allows collaborative teams to become the true engines of school improvement.

Become an Exemplary Role Model

The role school leaders play in a PLC is encapsulated by the mantra, "Do as I say *and* as I do." School leaders need to be mindful that they model the behaviors they expect to see staff demonstrate and understand the critical role this plays in building relational trust in their school. They must not only demonstrate high levels of integrity but also become exemplars of their school's collective commitments in their daily interactions with students, staff, and parents.

Meetings of the leadership team should be structured so that school leaders can execute actions and model similar processes that they expect collaborative teams to use. They must view themselves as the most important problem solvers in overcoming the challenges inherent to applying the PLC process in their school.

School leaders should also engage in ongoing cycles of action research and inquiry into the implementation of the PLC process at their school. Closely monitoring the impact of their actions on transforming their school into a high-performing PLC, they must problem solve to overcome issues as they arise so that their school's growth and improvement can continue.

Foster Cross-Team Collaboration

In high-performing and learning-focused PLCs, school leaders guarantee that collaborative teams can learn from one another. They explore and create opportunities that allow team leaders or facilitators and teams to regularly share teaching practices and approaches to build individual and collective practices.

These leaders share and scale up teaching practices that have the greatest impact on student learning—as discovered through the action research of collaborative teams—across their schools. To support a culture of continuous adult learning and improvement, leaders must understand student learning is strengthened when educators are constantly learning from one another and view their school's transformation into a PLC as an opportunity to enhance and maximize the results of continuous job-embedded professional learning.

Normalize Celebrations

Celebrating successes and acknowledging personal and collaborative growth helps the PLC process to stay on track and assists in motivating educators to continually strive toward achieving their goals. Without the strategic planning and commitment to build celebrations into the fabric of a school's PLC efforts, there can be a tendency for staff to revert to old ways of working, particularly when they feel overwhelmed, struggle to understand, or don't feel their efforts are being acknowledged.

Knowing this, school leaders must recognize the importance of celebration and monitor the work of teams to ensure individual and collective achievements are celebrated. They must also create opportunities for collaborative teams to share and celebrate these successes with other teams across the school, including the school's leadership team.

Staff meetings and professional learning forums, for example, can become vehicles for celebrating individual and team success.

A culture of private and public celebration and a genuine pride in achievements are mechanisms to propel individuals and teams to even higher levels of success. While celebrations are the responsibility of everyone within a PLC, they must be modeled constantly by school leaders.

Operationalize Team Norms

To ensure that collaborative teams are able to achieve high levels of learning for all students through their collaborative endeavors, school leaders should confirm that teams have designed team norms and critical behavior commitments to guide them when working together. Team norms are a team's agreed-on rules of engagement. As such, they must be expressed clearly and be written as specific behaviors rather than just as beliefs so that teams can accurately and actively monitor their adherence to them. The norms should also align with their school's collective commitments and clearly define the behavior expectations that teams set for themselves to maximize the effectiveness and productivity of their collaboration. By creating a healthy schoolwide culture of disciplined collaboration and a focus on continuous improvement, team members can hold themselves accountable to team norms before they hold others to them.

School leaders need to be realistic and understand that, regardless of team members' good intentions, when educators engage in rigorous and robust discussions, examine learning data related to the impact of their teaching, investigate ways to improve their teaching practice, and focus on improving student learning, infringements to norms are a natural consequence. As such, school leaders must ensure teams develop and agree on a clear norm-breach procedure to be implemented consistently when team norms are not adhered to. School leaders also need to support team leaders when continued infringements to norms occur by assisting them to deal with breaches and recognize that they may be called on as part of a collaborative team's tiered breach procedure.

It is important that school leaders maintain a positive mindset toward the ability of educators in their school to continually strengthen their collaborative endeavors. Appreciating that teams will continually develop and enhance their collaborative endeavors, school leaders can assist by ensuring that teams evaluate their adherence to norms at the conclusion of each collaborative team meeting and identify areas to continue to improve at subsequent meetings. This process supports teams to become more highly skilled in their collaborative endeavors as they continue to learn by doing.

As collaborative teams become more familiar with their work, school leaders can expect them to not only complete the actions and tasks necessary to improve the quality of their outcomes but also become more productive and efficient in doing so. To reflect and support this ongoing development, school leaders must ensure teams more formally evaluate their norms and adherence to them at least twice a year. The outcomes of these evaluations also allow school leaders to offer support and direct resources toward teams that are struggling or require further assistance to continue to strengthen their skills of collaboration.

Engage With and Commit to the Process

Just as collaborative teams need to focus their efforts on the right work, leadership teams need to focus their energy on the right areas. Doing so supports the ongoing growth of their school as a PLC and communicates to all stakeholders the non-negotiable commitments that everyone must make to the development of a learning-centered organization. As outlined in this chapter, communication is key to ensuring the foundations of a PLC are strong enough to allow collaborative teams to build their work on.

If we return to our analogy of a PLC being like an orange, the stronger that school leaders make the skin, the more protected the segments inside (teams) will be to develop and flourish.

Conclusion

Our aim in writing this book has been to share our combined expertise, developed through working with dedicated, motivated, and enthusiastic system and school leaders and educators as they too have become experts through experience. We desire to see other experts through experience emerge as they use, modify, and enhance the processes and approaches we have detailed in this book.

Our work in schools provides us with unique insight into the challenges and additional pressures that leaders and educators confront on a daily basis, which in many cases distract and shift them further from achieving the real objective that motivated them to enter the profession in the first place: to allow their students access to the enhanced future opportunities that a successful education affords.

All leaders and educators want to do the very best for the students they serve. Our aim is to assist and support leaders and educators by demystifying the PLC process and the work of collaborative teams to allow them to achieve high levels of learning for all their students. Through providing clarity about the right work, we aspire to support educators to reap the rewards for their daily hard work and endeavors.

As experts by experience, we know that what sits at the heart of any successful, high-performing PLC are strong and healthy collaborative teams that view the daily work they do in their classrooms as action research and part of ongoing cycles of inquiry that allow them to monitor the impact and strength of their teaching practice. Collaborative teams that work are also protected by the practices and culture of a thriving PLC and operate under the assumption that the key to improved learning for students is continuous job-embedded learning for educators. This professional learning is more impactful and relevant when educators work collaboratively to implement each cycle of learning.

Rather than being a recipe for success, we hope that *Collaborative Teams That Work* provides teams with a starting point for their collaborative endeavors and the opportunity to explore and learn about the actions and tasks that their collaborative endeavors must revolve around. As leaders and educators become experts by experience, we encourage them to learn from their action research and continue to strengthen and adapt the cycle of learning process to suit their school's unique context and needs.

For far too long, schools and educators have been tricked into believing that there is a magic bullet that if aimed and fired properly will solve all their problems. We believe that our greatest hope for improving student learning is recognizing and allowing leaders and educators to solve problems of practice with a process centered on collaborative action research. The cycle of learning process shifts the decision-making responsibility to teams, guiding and underpinning their collaborative endeavors as they become problem-solving teams. This process recognizes and centers the leading problem collaborative teams need to constantly strive to solve: "How can we strengthen our individual and collective teaching practice to ensure high levels of learning for all students?"

Working through each cycle of learning, educators benefit from job-embedded professional learning as they discuss, share, and learn about new and different ways of teaching while implementing each action and associated tasks as a team. The learning data they gather as part of this action research show whether their approaches are having the desired impact on student learning, validating the most highly effective for incorporation into their ongoing teaching practice.

So, in closing, we wish the next crop of experts by experience all the best in their endeavors as they place lived experience at the heart of their daily work and continuous research and learning. We remind you of the words of Carol Commodore (2014): "What we know today doesn't make yesterday wrong, it makes tomorrow better," and conclude with this encouraging maxim: "Anyone who has never made a mistake has never tried anything new" (BrainyQuote, n.d.).

We encourage you to continue being optimistic in your quest to achieve high levels of learning for all and to keep learning by doing.

Appendix A

Tips for Increasing Productivity in Collaborative Teams

Two Ways of Talking

Productive collaborative teams understand the importance of *purpose* to their dialogue. They know that at times they have to inquire into an issue to generate a collective understanding, while at other times they need to reach agreement on a course of action to take.

The work of Garmston and Wellman (2016) is very useful here. They delineate two types of conversation that, when learned and consciously applied to their work, can assist collaborative teams in working more efficiently. These two types of conversation are (1) dialogue and (2) discussion (Garmston & Wellman, 2016).

The core purpose of *dialogue* is understanding. In a collaborative team meeting, dialogue could be employed, for example, to collectively develop an understanding of the types of common preassessment that team members wish to implement at the beginning of their upcoming cycle of learning. A key element to dialogue is seeking to understand rather than be understood. In dialogue, each team member takes responsibility for ensuring all thinking is surfaced and considered in support of the process of inquiry.

In contrast, the core purpose of *discussion* is decision making. Discussion sees collaborative team members commit to actions, approaches, and processes that they believe, after due consideration, will give the best outcome. This consideration involves listening to alternative viewpoints in the quest to reach consensus, critical thinking, and deeper analysis of possible options. Symptoms of low-level discussion include team members reverting to what has always been done, the person with the highest position or loudest voice always winning out, or genuine ownership of and commitment to the course of action being absent.

It is important for schools to prioritize building the skills required to engage in productive collaboration through targeted professional learning, reflection, and monitoring. All the good intentions in the world won't amount to improvement in student learning if schools and teams don't operate in a way that is conducive to authentic inquiry—and carrying out the correct types of conversations is part of this. Collaborative team members are problem solvers, adopting and applying skills and tools that lead to successful learning outcomes. They solve problems by asking themselves and one another the right questions, and they allow these questions and their answers to guide their inquiry.

Productive collaborative teams skillfully weave both ways of talking into their meetings. At times they might spend more time in dialogue before engaging in discussion, while the opposite can occur at other times. Generally it comes down to the nature of the agenda item, its complexity, and where the team is in relation to that agenda item. For example, there is less complexity in agreeing to the day and time to administer preassessment than there is in determining the prioritized standards for a cycle of learning.

These two ways of talking lead to higher-quality solutions and a greater shared commitment to the ultimate decisions made by the team.

Protocols for Consensus Building

The process of inquiry requires team members to build consensus. Protocols are non-negotiable, high-leverage tools for collaborative teams that are genuine in their quest for higher levels of learning through consensus building.

We define *protocols* as predetermined sets or series of questions that govern team members' discussions as they work together within a given time frame. There are many instances in which protocols can be applied to the work of teams, including analyzing data, prioritizing actions, seeking ideas and understanding from research, reviewing team norms, examining underlying assumptions, differentiating fact from opinion, and developing a guaranteed and viable curriculum. The questions outlined within a protocol are often included on the meeting agenda to guide a team's discussions.

More information about protocols can be found in chapter 5 of *Transformative Collaboration: Five Commitments for Leading a Professional Learning Community* (Flanagan et al., 2016).

Skills for Inquiry

If skill is the ability to do something well and something that educators can develop, then being increasingly skillful is critical to the work of collaborative teams.

As a result of our extensive work with schools, we believe that the following are some of the most important skills for collaborative teams to hone. We have found the work of Thinking Collaborative to be particularly useful in this regard, particularly the skills outlined in the Adaptive Schools and Cognitive Coaching programs. (See https:// thinkingcollaborative.com for more information.)

1. Asking Inquiry Questions

Productive collaborative teams ask themselves the strongest and most relevant questions. The nature of these questions invites collective exploration and ensures the efficient use of team time. The criteria that teams use to ensure the questions they ask are genuinely useful to inquiry are as follows.

- Questions are open-ended, meaning that they can't be answered with a simple *yes* or *no* and often begin with the words *what* and *how*, rather than *can* or *should*. For example, "What types of assessment can apply here?" would be asked instead of "Should we use a short quiz?"

- Questions are plural in form to encourage many options to be put forward for exploration as opposed to only one. For example, "What types of assessments can we apply here?" would be asked instead of "What type of assessment can we use?"

- Questions are asked in an invitational tone to genuinely encourage team members to share their opinions, viewpoints, and ideas.

2. Paraphrasing

This skill involves summarizing the meaning of what someone has said, using different language to lead to greater clarity for themselves, the person whose ideas they have paraphrased, and other team members.

Paraphrasing is fundamentally a listening skill before it is a verbal skill. (Try paraphrasing something you didn't hear because you were too busy listening to your own thoughts.) Paraphrasing has the potential to capture the essence of someone's thinking, and can serve as a passport to cumulative idea generation when done well. The power of paraphrasing for collaborative teams is that it can lead to further inquiry. An example of paraphrasing is, "It's important for you that when we choose an assessment, it measures students' understanding beyond the standard as well as just up to it." This can then be followed by a question such as, "What might the assessment look like if we were to do that as a team?"

3. Pausing

Pausing is a gift to thinking. Mary Budd Rowe's (1986) pioneering research highlighted the importance of pausing to thinking. Thinking is both a prerequisite and benefit of inquiry. This is why pausing is so critical.

Embracing the pause as a way of creating the psychological space needed when feeling discomfort is important for teams. It sends the message to team members that what someone says is important enough to be considered and also provides those responding with time to collect their thoughts. Pausing can be used after a speaker has finished and before the next speaker responds. The amount of time to pause for will depend on the context and circumstance, but anywhere between three and ten seconds can be appropriate.

4. Being Self- and Team-Aware

When members are aware of the impact their contributions have on their collaborative team, alongside the impact that others' contributions have, that team increases its capacity to operate in a professional and disciplined manner.

Being self- and team-aware enables members to monitor the effectiveness of their dialogue and discussion and guides them in both what contributions they make in team meetings and how they make them. Heightening members' consciousness of what is said and how it is said builds productivity and supports teams to achieve their goals.

5. Assuming Positive Intent

Ensuring that team members focus on what binds them together rather than what divides them plays an important part in enhancing a team's productivity. Assuming positive intent supports the search for collaborative solutions to confronting issues by allowing team members to consider various viewpoints and disagree with one another without becoming combative.

When team members assume that their colleagues' intentions are good, teams are well placed to enhance their collaborative conversations. As an example, consider how you might respond to a colleague expressing concern about an assessment item you've suggested. If you assume that your team member's intentions are positive and constructive, you might ask, "Can you share more about your concerns?" However, if the assumption of positive intent is absent, you might feel defensive and be inclined to respond, "We don't have time to be negative. Can we just decide on something?"

Appendix B

Sample Collaborative Team Meeting Agenda Template

Meeting Date	Team	Attendees	Team Roles
			Chairperson: Minute-taker: Norm-observer: Timekeeper:

Team Norms	Norm-Breach Procedure
Time: Decision making: Participation: Listening: Confidentiality: Expectations:	
Refer to the supplementary norm document for a full list of shared beliefs and agreed behaviors to be demonstrated at all meetings.	

Critical PLC Questions	Guiding Questions
1. What do we want our students to learn? 2. How will we know our students are learning? 3. How will we respond when some students do not learn? 4. How will we extend the learning for students who are already proficient? (DuFour et al., 2016)	1. What student learning issue are we seeking to address? 2. How will we know we have addressed the student learning issue? 3. How might we overcome the issue? 4. What actions will we trial? 5. Which actions will we now adopt to enrich our instructional practices?
	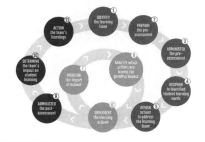

Item		Time Allocation	Decisions
Establish a focus norm.		Two minutes	
Review the actions agreed to at the last meeting.		Three minutes	
Learning focus items	1.		
	2.		
	3.		
	4.		
	5.		
	6.		
	7.		
	8.		
Allocate roles for the next meeting.		One minute	Chairperson: Minute-taker: Norm-observer: Timekeeper:
Develop items for the next meeting's agenda.		Two minutes	
Review the decisions made in the meeting.		Two minutes	
Review the focus norm.		Two minutes	

Read-Only Items

Item	Team Member

Upcoming Events

Date	Event

Figure B.1: Sample collaborative team meeting agenda template.

*Visit **go.SolutionTree.com/PLCbooks** for a free reproducible version of this figure.*

References

Allensworth, E. M., & Hart, H. (2018). *How do principals influence student achievement?* Chicago: University of Chicago Consortium on School Research. Accessed at https://consortium.uchicago.edu/sites /default/files/2018-10/Leadership%20Snapshot-Mar2018-Consortium.pdf on December 30, 2020.

Assess. (n.d.) In *Online Etymonline Dictionary.* Accessed at https://etymonline.com/word/assess on July 24, 2020.

Black, P., & Wiliam, D. (1998). Inside the black box: Raising standards through classroom assessment. *Phi Delta Kappan, 80*(2), 144, 146–148.

BrainyQuote. (n.d.). Albert *Einstein quotes.* Accessed at www.brainyquote.com/quotes/albert_einstein_109012.

Buffum, A., Mattos, M., & Weber, C. (2012). *Simplifying response to intervention: Four essential guiding principles.* Bloomington, IN: Solution Tree Press.

Clarke, S. (2001). *Unlocking formative assessment: Practical strategies for enhancing pupils' learning in the primary classroom.* London: Hodder Education.

Collins, J. (2001). *Good to great: Why some companies make the leap. . . and others don't.* New York: Harper Business.

Commodore, C. [@CarolCommodore]. (2014, August 1). *What we know today doesn't make yesterday wrong, it makes tomorrow better.* [Tweet]. Accessed at https://twitter.com/CarolCommodore /status/495253940145901568 on December 30, 2020.

Cotton, K. (1988, May). *Monitoring student learning in the classroom.* Washington, DC: Office of Educational Research and Improvement. Accessed at https://files.eric.ed.gov/fulltext/ED298085 .pdf on March 24, 2021.

DuFour, R., DuFour, R., & Eaker, R. (2009). *Revisiting Professional Learning Communities at Work: New insights for improving schools.* Melbourne, Australia: Hawker Brownlow Education.

DuFour, R., DuFour, R., Eaker, R., & Many, T. W. (2006). *Learning by doing: A handbook for Professional Learning Communities at Work* (1st ed.). Bloomington, IN: Solution Tree Press.

DuFour, R., DuFour, R., Eaker, R., Many, T. W., & Mattos, M. (2016). *Learning by doing: A handbook for Professional Learning Communities at Work* (3rd. ed.). Bloomington, IN: Solution Tree Press.

DuFour, R., DuFour, R., Eaker, R., Many, T. W., & Mattos, M. (with G. Grift & C. Sloper). (2017). *Learning by doing: A handbook for Professional Learning Communities at Work* (Rev. Australian ed.). Melbourne, Australia: Hawker Brownlow Education.

Flanagan, T., Grift, G., Lipscombe, K., Sloper, C., & Wills, J. (2016). *Transformative collaboration: Five commitments for leading a professional learning community.* Melbourne, Australia: Hawker Brownlow Education.

Garmston, R. J., & Wellman, B. M. (2016). *The adaptive school: A sourcebook for developing collaborative groups* (3rd ed.). Lanham, MD: Rowman & Littlefield.

Great Schools Partnership. (2013, August 29). *Summative assessment.* Accessed at https://www.edglossary .org/summative-assessment on December 30, 2020.

Grift, G., & Major, C. (2020). *Teachers as architects of learning: Twelve constructs to design and configure successful learning experiences* (2nd ed.). Bloomington, IN: Solution Tree Press.

Hargreaves, A., & Fullan, M. (2012). *Professional capital: Transforming teaching in every school.* New York: Teachers College Press.

Harris, A. (2014). *Distributed leadership matters: Perspectives, practicalities, and potential.* Thousand Oaks, CA: Corwin.

Hattie, J. (2012). *Visible learning for teachers: Maximizing impact on learning.* New York: Routledge.

Hattie, J. (2015). The applicability of Visible Learning to higher education. *Scholarship of Teaching and Learning in Psychology, 1*(1), 79–91. Accessed at http://dx.doi.org/10.1037/stl0000021 on December 30, 2020.

Hockett, J. A., & Doubet, K. J. (2013). Turning on the lights: What pre-assessments can do. *Educational Leadership, 71*(4), 50–54.

Izadi, S. (2018). *The kindness method: Change your habits for good using self-compassion and understanding.* Basingstoke, England: Pan Macmillan.

Jensen, B., Hunter, J., Sonnemann, J., & Cooper, S. (2014, March). *Making time for great teaching.* Melbourne, Australia: Grattan Institute. Accessed at https://grattan.edu.au/wp-content /uploads/2014/03/808-making-time-for-great-teaching.pdf on January 4, 2021.

Kim, H., & Care, E. (2018, March 27). *Learning progressions: Pathways for 21st century teaching and learning* [Blog post]. Accessed at https://www.brookings.edu/blog/education-plus-development /2018/03/27/learning-progressions-pathways-for-21st-century-teaching-and-learning on January 4, 2021.

Marzano, R. J. (2017). *The new art and science of teaching.* Bloomington, IN: Solution Tree Press.

Marzano, R. J., Heflebower, T., Hoegh, J. K., Warrick, P. B., & Grift, G. (with L. Hecker & J. Wills). (2016). *Collaborative teams that transform schools: The next step in PLCs.* Melbourne, Australia: Hawker Brownlow Education.

Marzano, R. J., Warrick, P. B., Rains, C. L., & DuFour, R. (2018). *Leading a High Reliability School.* Bloomington, IN: Solution Tree Press.

Marzano, R. J., Warrick, P. B., & Simms, J. A. (2014). *A handbook for High Reliability Schools: The next step in school reform* (Rev. Australian ed.). Melbourne, Australia: Hawker Brownlow Education.

Mattos, M., DuFour, R., DuFour, R., Eaker, R., & Many, T. W. (with G. Grift & C. Sloper). (2019). *Concise answers to frequently asked questions about Professional Learning Communities at Work* (Rev. Australian ed.). Melbourne, Australia: Hawker Brownlow Education.

Mitroff, I. I., & Sagasti, F. (1973). Epistemology as general systems theory: An approach to the design of complex decision-making experiments. *Philosophy of the Social Sciences, 3*(2), 117–134. Accessed at https://doi.org/10.1177/004839317300300202 on January 4, 2021.

O'Neill, J., & Conzemius, A. (2006). *The power of SMART goals: Using goals to improve student learning.* Bloomington, IN: Solution Tree Press.

Prosser, B., Lucas, B., & Reid, A. (Eds.). (2010). *Connecting lives and learning: Renewing pedagogy in the middle years.* Adelaide, Australia: Wakefield Press.

Rowe, M. B. (1986). Wait time: Slowing down may be a way of speeding up! *Journal of Teacher Education, 37*(1), 43–50. Accessed at https://doi.org/10.1177/002248718603700110 on January 4, 2021.

Sagor, R. (2000). *Guiding school improvement with action research.* Alexandria, VA: Association for Supervision and Curriculum Development.

Sanders, W. L., Wright, S. P., & Horn, S. P. (1997). Teacher and classroom context effects on student achievement: Implications for teacher evaluation. *Journal of Personnel Evaluation in Education, 11*(1), 57–67. Accessed at https://doi.org/10.1023/A:1007999204543 on January 4, 2021.

Taba H., & Elkins, D. (1966). *Teaching strategies for the culturally disadvantaged.* Chicago: Rand McNally.

Tomlinson, C. A., & McTighe, J. (2006). *Integrating differentiated instruction and Understanding by Design: Connecting content and kids.* Alexandria, VA: Association for Supervision and Curriculum Development.

State Government of Victoria. (2020, November 18). *Understand your impact on student learning growth.* Accessed at https://www.education.vic.gov.au/school/teachers/teachingresources/practice /improve/Pages/eitimpact.aspx on January 4, 2021.

Testari. (n.d.). In *WordSense Dictionary online.* Accessed at https://www.wordsense.eu/testari/ on September 11, 2020.

Timperley, H. (2009, August 17). *Using assessment data for improving teaching practice.* Paper presented at the Australian Council for Educational Research's Assessment and Student Learning: Collecting, Interpreting and Using Data to Inform Teaching Conference, Perth, Australia.

Weber, C., Hierck, T., & Larson, G. (with C. Sloper & G. Grift). (2016). *Collaborative systems of support: Learning for all.* Melbourne, Australia: Hawker Brownlow Education.

Weimer, M. (2008, December 16). Effective teaching strategies: The importance of marrying content and process. *Faculty Focus.* Accessed at https://facultyfocus.com/articles/effective-teaching -strategies/effective-teaching-strategies-the-importance-of-marrying-content-and-process on January 4, 2021.

Index